SCARS

THANKFUL, NOT SHAKEN

OVERCOMING ANXIETY AND ABUSE

Nikki A. Edwards

TRILOGY CHRISTIAN PUBLISHERS
TUSTIN, CA

Trilogy Christian Publishers
A Wholly Owned Subsidary of Trinity Broadcasting Network
2442 Michelle Drive
Tustin, CA 92780

For information, address Trilogy Christian Publishing

Rights Department, 2442 Michelle Drive, Tustin, Ca 92780.

Trilogy Christian Publishing/ TBN and colophon are trademarks of Trinity Broadcasting Network.

For information about special discounts for bulk purchases, please contact Trilogy Christian Publishing.

Manufactured in the United States of America

10 9 8 7 6 5 4 3 2 1

Library of Congress Cataloging-in-Publication Data is available.

ISBN 978-1-64088-595-0

ISBN 978-1-64088-596-7 (ebook)

Contents

Dedication

This book is dedicated to my handsome husband who has always been my rock, along with being so supportive from the very beginning of our marriage to encourage me to follow my dreams writing my book. You have been an inspiration in my life and taught me what it feels like to experience real love and compassion. Also, I want to give big kisses to my three beautiful children and my God-daughter who I adore so much. Mommy loves you more than anything in the world. Thank each of you for being patient with me on my journey writing this tough book – it is well needed to inspire others in life. I love you all so much.

Acknowledgement

I want to acknowledge all my sweet sisters in Christ that have been through this journey with me. Some of you have been with me since we were in elementary school; some have been with me during the lowest times in my life; some have been in my life since I accepted Jesus Christ as my Lord and Savior; and others came later in my adulthood being a wife and a mother. Each of you ladies mean the absolute world to me.

Thank you for the special team that worked and/or were volunteers with Trinity Baptist Church in Yukon, OK that dedicated their time to help and to show me guidance I needed the most with my walk with Christ when I became a Christian at the age of 15.

Richie and Susan Fisher were the youth pastors on staff at the time and my neighbors as well. Thank you both for all you have done to be amazing leaders in the beginning of my life finding Christ and never giving up on me and my siblings.

Stacy Baker and Denise Miller were my D-Team Leaders and mentors who volunteered their time to show me love, acceptance, encouragement, and compassion; not looking down upon me with all the battles and scars I went through. Thank you for never giving up on me. Thank you, Denise Miller, for being there for me when I went through a trying time with my marriage. Thank you, Stacy Baker, for leading me in the right direction to find the right Publisher for me with Trilogy Christian Publishing company, and taking the time to read my book to give me feedback and encouragement that I am doing God's will for my life and for others to find hope like I did.

Thank you to my parents for everything they were able to provide for me in my youth. Even though we may have had a difficult life together when I was young, I have still learned from the circumstances I was in and it has taught me a great deal of life and what is important. Through my life challenges, it has made me the woman I am today that is strong, fighter, courageous, woman of God, Princess warrior, survivor of wrath and overcomer. I love you both dearly. God has done miracles for you both and brought you to Jesus Christ as your Lord and Savior. That is all I can ask for.

Introduction

Anxiety, worry, fear...everywhere you look, people are struggling to survive emotionally, mentally, and physically. We all have different problems and circumstances. Whether it is a doctor's appointment that had a bad outcome, a child who has broken your heart, or concern that has gripped your feelings, life never stops. Furthermore, it isn't fair. It seems no one, not even a child, is off limits from the evil that roams in this world. What can we do? How will we keep from literally worrying ourselves to death?

As someone who survived extreme circumstances, I have faced my days and nights of fear. I hope by sharing my story, reflecting on what God has to say, and walking together through what He has taught me, that you will be able to truly *Unload Your Worries*.

Unload Your Worries

1 Peter 5:6-7 says, "So humble yourselves under the mighty power of God, and at the right time he will lift you up in honor. Give all your worries and cares to God, for he cares about you" (NLT).

We need to look for the hidden treasures; our treasures are found in God. The answers are in His Word and His messages remain in the Bible. Each thought you have, or feeling you receive from Him, is the Holy Spirit speaking to you. God has given you the wisdom and knowledge to find the key to His answers. We need to be silent and listen. Look deep in your soul and find rest. God has called upon us to look underneath the baggage of clutter in our minds and set them free to see clarity of His vision for our lives.

I can feel my heart beating and pounding against my chest and the blood in my veins is racing through. Every breath I take I breathe the air of God that gives me life here on earth so we can discover the meaning of life.

God prevails in us and waits patiently while He puts hidden treasures of His secrets in us so we can be transformed by his beauty here on earth. God does speak profoundly to not fear evil but fear only God. He will protect and guide our every thought, and direct our journey to the green pastures. He will bring forth a whole new understanding in you, so you don't miss the answers of His richness with the path of righteousness.

Anoint me Father of the oil that covers my head of your goodness and mercy on me. Direct my path of Your righteousness toward Your never-ending happiness.

Continue to search God's Word. Pay attention and listen quietly for His wisdom. When a storm arises in your life don't let that storm destroy you. Scream to the storm that your God is bigger than it is. Give all your worries and anxieties to God and let Him take authority over all strength and weakness. He will lead you to the new road that won't be bumpy because He has prepared your new beginnings and destinations of your future travel.

Trust and rely on God and His Word. Grab a hold of Jesus' hand and let Him lead you to a clean and stable road. Let God clean anything that appears on your road. Let Him dust off the mess for you and allow Him to carry any garbage that comes your way. He is the King of all Kings and He is our Head and we are His body of Christ. So let God's knowledge bring a new wisdom of understanding.

If you follow God's will then God will bless you with an abundance of happiness. Give everything to Him and he will tell you what your next move will be. He is preparing the season of your harvest of His glory. Be magnified in His name; we are His children and He is our Father. Let God discipline and teach us what we need to know to get ready.

Brothers and sisters, I do not consider myself yet to
have taken hold of it. But one thing I do: Forgetting
what is behind and straining toward what is ahead,
I press on toward the goal to win the prize for which
God has called me heavenward in Christ Jesus.

Philippians 3:13-14, NIV

The decision is up to us to take the step of faith and to let
go of the things that are causing us to be distracted: being successful, always needing to feel wanted by others, to prove to
people that we are someone of importance. But the truth is the
only person we need to prove it to is Jesus Christ our Lord and
Savior.

As we close our eyes to pray and meditate on God's mercy,
ask God to be with you every single day. Speak boldly to your
Heavenly Father to give you the encouragement while you are
here on earth so you can be used as a disciple. Do it with obe-
dience and a willingness to be used by Him, to be confronted
when we are making wrong decisions, and to be a mentor to
others.

The Book of Ruth in the Bible has a wonderful story of Naomi being a mentor to Ruth. Naomi's name was Mara, which
meant bitterness, because she had a bad life and made some
bad decisions along her journey. Later she changed and became a wise, older woman to lead a faithful girl, Ruth. Ruth lost
her husband, but Ruth had an incredible amount of faith and
she trusted God to allow Naomi to guide her daughter-in-law.

In Ruth 1:16 (NIV), Ruth replied, "Don't urge me to leave you or turn back from you. Wherever you go, I will go, and where you stay I will stay. Your people will be my people and your God my God. ." It's an incredible story of Ruth's dedication of her whole life to Naomi, her mother-in-law.

I know some people may feel like Naomi, wanting to guide and teach others to live with abundance of joy.

MISSING GOD'S MESSAGE

I know there will be many days we will be praying over and over, asking God to speak to our souls or let us to hear His voice. We beg God to speak louder than the devil's voice so we can only concentrate on His words and not miss the message that God is speaking to us.

> Yet the Lord longs to be gracious to you; therefore he will rise up to show you compassion. For the Lord is a God of Justice. Blessed are all who wait for him!
>
> Isaiah 30:18, NIV

Tell God you are waiting and listening to Him more profoundly and deeply than ever before. Ask God to prepare you to serve Him and only Him. Take away all the distractions, worrying what your peer's think or say, but only what He is revealing to your soul. Seek your faith and trust knowing God will provide your needs. Let Him know that He is teaching us to be strong. Speak the words out loud.

My help comes from the Lord, the Maker of heaven and earth. He will not let your foot slip—he who watches over you will not slumber.

Psalm 121:2-3 NIV

Cry out to the Lord that you are longing for your destination to arrive on course so He can start the beginning stages preparing you. Lord, as we ask You to develop knowledge in our everyday life to grow more in tune with You, help us to see Your vision and make it clear as the water so there won't be any misunderstanding.

I know how to be abased, and I know how to abound. Everywhere and in all things, I have learned both to be full and to be hungry, both to be abound and to suffer need. I can do all things through Christ who strengthens me.

Philippians 4:12-13, NKJV

Another translation with the NLT reads:

I know how to live on almost nothing or with everything. I have learned the secret of living in every situation, whether it is with a full stomach or empty, with plenty or little. For I can do everything through Christ, who gives me strength.

Many of us in life are praying for God's mercy to not suffer anymore, and to take away financial burdens; to have a successful career, and to take away our fears of worry that are constantly overtaking our minds. Ask God to reveal in your heart to know He is a loving and gentle God that is a provider for His children.

> Trust in the Lord with all your heart and lean not on
> your own understanding; in all your ways submit to
> him, and he will make your paths straight.
> Proverbs 3:5-6, NIV

If you ever feel in constant turmoil, or feel backed up against the wall from the fear paralyzing you by not knowing what steps to take, or questioning yourself if you are making the right decision or if it is God speaking to you. Close your eyes, take a deep breath, and exhale to calm your mind. Get down on your hands and knees, then let God speak to your soul while silence is around you to hear His voice. Go humbly before Him in strength and bravery, asking Him for perseverance. We all need God's grace and confidence to sustain the trials in life so we can grow in His teachings over our lives.

> But he said to me, "My grace is sufficient for you, for
> my power is made perfect in weakness." Therefore, I
> will boast all the more gladly about my weaknesses,
> so that Christ's power may rest on me. That is why,
> for Christ's sake, I delight in weaknesses, in insults,

in hardships, in persecutions, in difficulties. For when I am weak, then I am strong.

2 Corinthians 12:9-10, NIV

All we need to do right now is replenish our souls to God instead of serving idols of this world that don't matter.

Brothers and sisters, I do not consider myself yet to have taken hold of it. But one thing I do: Forgetting what is behind and straining toward what is ahead.

Philippians 3:13, NIV

Let God break down those walls of apprehension in your heart, and fear and anxieties that try to triumph your soul. Go alone before God and worship Him. I know it might not be easy to be alone, but know when you are struggling and feeling down or the need for someone else to take you out of the pits. All we need to remember is Christ our Lord and Savior is the only source of complete fulfillment.

Seek his will in all you do, and he will show you which path to take.

Proverbs 3:6, NLT

Prayer:

Jesus, we give our lives to You, Lord with open arms of surrender and compassion that You will restore our souls of brokenness that we have felt for many years. Restore our minds and consciousness that we will abide only in Your understandings and not of our own. We trust you with our lives into Your hands that You will completely banish all the things of devil lurking in or around us. We ask that You rebuke the devil out of our souls and take over him with Your glory of righteousness. We listen quietly for Your word daily. We give all our fleshly desires to You. Grant us the strength and serenity to go through the waiting period with joy.

There will be a time in our lives that we will have to make the decision to do a full 180-degree transformation of the mind, body and soul. We cannot stay still with old behaviors, but we must graduate into a new way of thinking. This will take a lot of time, patience, hard work; and sweat, blood, and tears to make this transformation happen. It takes dedication and the desire to make a difference.

There will be storms that will reveal lies of the enemy that will try to speak to your soul to distract you from what God has in store for you. We will have to deal with any fear, anxiety, or doubt that crosses our path. We must face our fears head on and surrender everything to God. We need to go before the Lord and ask Him to glorify Himself in us, and ask Christ to have His way in us to be able to submit with all authority over everything we do, say, or touch.

> Therefore, I urge you, brothers and sisters, in view of God's mercy, to offer your bodies as a living sacrifice, holy and pleasing to God—this is your true and proper worship.
>
> Romans 12:1, NIV

We must have a zero tolerance of the devil with his scheming ways. Let's agree to put to death the flesh thoughts that try to surpass God's passion over our lives by renewing our minds and transforming our bodies to worship and to shut the door of fear or rejection in our lives. Take all authority and put it under your feet. Speak truth in your mind and when fear arises up in your body you will have the maturity to recognize it is the devil. You will cast out the enemy that he does not have a hold of you, and he cannot steal your peace any longer. The only way he can is if you let him.

Prayer:

My precious King of All Kings please help us to have the complexity of our hearts that will be risen to you Oh Father, full of love, and to be restored from our broken hearts, so you can use us for Your will. Help us to quit questioning Your ability to heal us, but help us to be silent and still for Your Kingdom.

> In addition to all this, take up the shield of faith, with which you can extinguish all the flaming arrows of the evil one.
>
> Ephesians 6:16 NIV

We need to cry out to Jesus to make us brave through all the trials that come our way.

GOING THROUGH THE PREPARATION

> I waited patiently for the LORD; he turned to me and heard my cry. He lifted me out of the slimy pit, out of the mud and mire; he set my feet on a rock and gave me a firm place to stand. He put a new song in my mouth, a hymn of praise to our God. Many will see and fear the LORD and put their trust in him.
>
> Psalm 40:1-3, NIV

I was reading a book by T.D. Jakes, *Can You Stand to Be Blessed?* He spoke about the real test of faith in facing the silence of being on hold. Those are the suspended times of indecision. There will be times God might not tell us yes or no; He might say, "not right now my little one." God wants to bless us so much more than we can ever imagine. He wants to teach us to calm down and quit being in a hurry for our destiny to come. If we rush it, it may not be as exciting or fulfilling as we may have thought. If we just wait for the Lord to say, "Go my sweet one," that gives us a more rewarding feeling because He was right beside us the entire time, holding our hand with the purist direction on the path of righteousness He intended us to be on.

DECEPTION FROM THE ENEMY

Women or Young Ladies: if you feel like you are being put into a position to rush into a relationship by getting married, or moving in with each other before marriage, you must give it to God. Let Him direct you when, where, and how to be guided by the right truth what is right from God. Don't let your selfish needs overtake what is the right way of living for God.

To give you a background of my life, here are some trials I endured. I wish I could have had someone there for me to direct me on the right healthy path of thinking.

Many times in my life I made terrible decisions with relationships. I was neglected as a child and I had a huge gap in my heart that I felt like it needed to be fulfilled by having a boy's attention or love. I allowed the affections to distract me from what was the most important feeling of harmony with God, and what true love really is. We are God's bride. He wants to take care of all our needs. If you feel forced into making a decision to please a man, then you know that it is not of God. That is of the devil.

The ability to understand our own needs is a challenge. God created us here on earth not for ourselves, but for the purpose of others, by encouraging them to make right decisions in life. Our destiny is predetermined. God has guided us to a destination of completion. We must be hungry for more of God, not of the attention of men to feel completed.

Prayer:

God, we come humbly before You to ask for Your Holy Spirit to blow the wind in the direction where You want us to turn for our freedom of feeling needed or wanted. Help us not be bound of the devil's deception, but set us free from any tribulations. Help us to connect our hearts and souls for the deliberation, and to declare war on the enemy. Help us to build a shield of faith that the enemy cannot move our wall of the honor for our Most High. Help us to reclaim our vision to another level for You.

"For I know the plans I have for you," says the LORD. "They are plans for good and not for disaster, to give you a future and a hope."

Jeremiah 29:11, NLT

My sweet friends, God's mind is full of You. Even in those moments of absolute stagnation in your life. He is working an expected end for your good. I know many times in life the silence and the fear overtake our ability to move. We may feel we have been punched in the stomach, and our breath got knocked out of us. We may feel shaken by the enemy, but the quench of the thirst for more of You, God, is stronger. We may get blinded by the not knowing, and we may allow it to overtake our hearts. We may even feel our hearts working overtime and pounding when the devil tries to attack us more frequently. The devil may think the blow he tried would knock us out, but we are much stronger than we can ever imagine. He thought he would overtake us, but he was wrong because our hearts are strong, and we have the protection of God's hand over every beat of our heart that is pumping full of God's blood through our veins.

Blessed *are* the pure in heart, for they shall see God.

Matthew 5:8, NKJV

We must be aware that God's fullest sense of protection is over our lives and that He will take our inabilities and fleshly desires away. The Book of David cries out to God.

Create in me a pure heart, O God, and renew a steadfast spirit within me.

Psalm 51:10, NIV

The Greek word *Katharos*, means "to clean out." The definition by NAS New Testament Greek Lexicon:

1. Clean, pure
   a. Physically
      1. Purified by fire
      2. In similitude, like a vine cleansed by pruning and so fitted to bear fruit
   b. In a Levitical sense
      1. Clean, the use of which is not forbidden, imparts no uncleanness
   c. Ethically
      1. Free from corrupt desire, from sin and guilt
      2. Free from every admixture of what is false, sincere genuine
      3. Blameless, innocent
      4. Unstained with the guilt of anything

CHRIST THE PERFECT ONE

> All these many people who have had faith in God are
> around us like a cloud. Let us put every thing out of
> our lives that keeps us from doing what we should.
> Let us keep running in the race that God has planned
> for us.
>
> Hebrews 12:1, NLV

Prayer:

*In the course of this action that we feel in our hearts, we pronounce
to you O' God, that You will cleanse us with the Holy water and purify
our hearts and souls. We leave the old us behind in the water, and rise
the with new us out as we confess that You are the Lord of our lives, and
that You gave Your only Son to die for our sins. That You raised Him
from the dead and now we are saved by the sweet breath of air that You
breathed in us to cool the instant burning flames that dissipate out of
our bodies. You have healed us, Jesus, with all our sins, and gave us a
new life to walk. Help us to honor You and glorify Your love over us with
the new vision to accomplish what we need to do. Help us not to waste
any more time here on earth. Give us the power and privilege to do Your
will. We cry out to You God stating, "Today is the day we will never be
the same again!" This will be a new year that we will be refreshed and
awakened from our enemy; that Your angels will surround us with Your
protection. Condition us to have the understanding and the clarity so
we can prevent any more harm over our lives. Enlighten our hearts, Jesus, that we will never forget. In Jesus' name, Amen.*

THE NEW SEASON OF LIFE IN TRAINING

Another quote paraphrased in this book, Peaks & Valleys *Can You Stand to Be Blessed?*, by T.D. Jakes:

> "It speaks about a farmer building a harvest, "like the ground that has given much and received little, you need to be broken and turned over, allowed to rest for a time, and prepared for the next season of the yield."

We must remember to thank God in that He has given us a chance to rest and heal, so He can better prepare us for our next season in life. If we work too hard, we can run low on fuel and eventually get burned out. God gives us a chance to clear our minds and prepare for the next harvest in our life. Let's say the farmer built incredible harvest, then winter comes and destroys all the crops. Does the Farmer just throw his hands up in the air and say, "I quit," and give up? No, he starts preparing for the next season and pulls out all the old damaged crops, then begins to plant new seeds in the ground. While the seeds are resting in the soil until spring comes, then you will see all the new hard work that was done by the farmer. You will see the new crops start to flourish and grow beautifully from all the preparation that was put into it by the farmer.

This is how our lives are. When we are resting, we still must learn to prosper and grow for the next season. Mordecai was a gentleman who prepared Queen Ester to have a blessing. She was a very poor woman who was called to become a Queen. She had to learn to prepare her mind to be counseled, so she was able to teach from her heart and spirit to go deeper in her mind to reach the level God wanted her to be at. God gives us patience prepare us for the empowerment of His Glory.

> That person is like a tree planted by streams of water, which yields its fruit in season and whose leaf does not wither—whatever they do prospers.
>
> Psalm 1:3, NIV

If we pay more attention, we may feel like we are waiting for a long time to see God's results sown. God is telling us to just wait until the time has come where we now can reap His harvest.

Prayer:

We thank you Jesus for giving us time to rest and learn. Give us the vision to see things beyond our expectations of your glory, in your Mighty Name I pray Amen.

Ultimately, every day is a choice, decision, feeling; and a complexity of difficult issues that arise along our paths. When we go through difficult times in our lives, the devil seems to destroy our peace, joy, and happiness. Right now, we may feel like we are going through a mix of emotions from frustrated, anxious, depressed, offended, annoyed, irritated and/or confused with our lives. We must remind ourselves every day when we walk that we must make the constant effort to know that what God is saying to us is His truth. Please do not get mixed up with the enemy's lies he tries to throw our way. We must learn to clear our minds and pray diligently that we are being led by God. Don't let bad thoughts provoke your decision-making. Remind yourself daily these feelings will pass and they're only temporary.

If you must, scream out loud in the name of Jesus and cast out all bad thoughts that come to your mind. There will be times in your life you just want to scream at the top of your lungs, pull your hair out, and want to give up and say, "I am done." But God doesn't want that for us. We may feel like a failure and alone in this process. However, you are not the only one going through this constant battle with the enemy. Go before Jesus and reclaim those bad thoughts and give them back to Him. Ask God to reconcile your ability to overcome the thoughts that are lingering around you to be able to clear your mind.

Prayer:

My precious King, we need you more than anything in this world of heartache. When darkness comes our way, we ask of You to take away the worries and pressures we feel inside that we are not good enough. Help us to sit still so we can allow Your peace to come over us to break down the anxieties of wrong thinking. You are the truth, Lord. We come in silence to ask for Your guidance to allow Your overflowing cup of love in our hearts. In the name of Jesus, we won't allow the devil to draw confusion in our hearts. Help us to quit worrying and allow our minds to be completely restored. In your precious Heavenly name, Amen.

SEEKING GOD'S KNOWLEDGE OF WISDOM

There have been days in my past that I contemplated whether I was hearing God's word. Is this really you Lord clear as day speaking to my soul? There will be moments when I am searching for that missing piece that feels like I am in the desert trying to find that pinpoint of treasure that I can dig up and unravel the puzzle of His calling for me to hear. Question after question, waiting for the unanswered prayers. I must humble myself to you, Lord, to not doubt of Your plan for my life. There will be days traveling in the dry desert with no food or water to survive on, then I turn around and I will see running water in the middle of the dry desert that seems too far away to travel to, to provide my dying body the water it needs to replenish my thirst and strength to continue on. I am sure you have felt this way before. It may not feel fun, and it may seem unbearable at times in your life, but we must continue even when our bodies don't want to go on fighting.

Prayer:

Lord, we come to You, asking for Your satisfaction knowing we are truly hearing the right thoughts and desires of You. Help us not to eat rich meats of the world's table. Help us not to partake in anything that would be harmful to our bodies that our flesh wants. Give us the strength to not be frightened about our journey and the obstacles we will hit along the way. Help our conversations always be filled with grace and love, so we know how to answer someone else's hurts when asked to pray for them. In Your holy name, Amen.

Being a faithful servant for God is not always easy in life. We must constantly remind ourselves to be humble and not prideful. Remember our lives have been predetermined for our future by God. He has a purpose for us while we are living among this world to be faithful to Him, and teach people to believe in Jesus so they can be delivered to live forever in all eternity in Heaven with our Savior. God gives us discernment in the knowledge of His all-powerful ways. He knows the hidden secrets of the darkness. We must open our eyes to see what He is trying to show us. There will be hidden things that will pass of this world through the darkness of sin. Seasons have been changed; Kings are disposed of their lives. Many people in life are selfish and worry about themselves only, instead of worrying for others that are lost and need to know who Jesus is.

To those who listen to my teaching, more understanding will be given, and they will have an abundance of knowledge. But for those who are not listening, even what little understanding they have will be taken away from them.

Matthew 13:12, NLT

2

Rejected

These are the eyes of a little girl who felt dread inside. At a very young age, I was left alone many nights to take care of my little brother by myself. My mom worked nights and when my dad got home from working hard labor with concrete, he would come home and start drinking throughout the night. He became extremely mean and sometimes violent with my mother when she would come home from working a long shift at a waitress job.

I remember my mom crying and not being happy. I know she would drink just to deal with my father and his outbursts of emotion when he was drinking heavily. Many nights I would be so frightened and feel alone. I was so little. I didn't know what I could do to help my mom. There were many nights that led to my father passed out on the couch.

One night when my little brother was a baby he needed his diaper changed. My dad and my grandpa were drinking heavily all day, which led them both to pass out. They wouldn't wake up from their stupor. I eventually had to change my little brother's diaper. I was only four years old. I remember I couldn't get the diaper on right. I was crying and my brother was crying. We passed out asleep from being so exhausted from the stress we endured.

My grandma Ruth came to the house and woke us up where we had fallen asleep on my parents' bed. She came to our rescue and took care of us while waiting for my mother to come home from a long day at work.

There were many frightening nights I had to experience. My father would hit my mother and abuse her. One night he restricted her airway until she lost consciousness. I was screaming and crying trying to wake her up. I thought my mother was dead. When my mother finally woke up, she called the police on my father. He got arrested and taken to jail. The police officers came inside my house and my dad pretended to be asleep and they went into his room to get him out of bed. They handcuffed my father right in front of me. That was such a devastating moment to experience at such a young age.

There was one night that their fight got so bad my mother couldn't take it much more and she hit my dad in the head with his work boot. Then the police came and they both got arrested and taken to jail for domestic violence.

The day after the incident happened, my grandma Ruth took us to jail to go pick up my mother. There were so many days she came over to help us out. Thank you, Jesus, for sending her to us when we needed her, at our most vulnerable age of life. We were little innocent children who didn't have a meaning of life or know what security felt like.

My father got worse when his sister committed suicide in June of 1993. He was not emotionally strong enough to handle the loss of his little sister. He took it very hard. He started to drink more and more, and eventually it became every day, then all day long. When he did go to work, he would drink on the job with all his other buddies. I remember my father just being mad, depressed, hot headed, or passed out from being drunk.

My dad couldn't control his drinking. He got multiple DUI's that led him to spend time in jail for months to years at a time, so we were left without a father off and on from 1994-2004, and our mother had to work all the time to keep a roof over our heads.

We took in two out of the three of my aunt's children. The other child was three years old when she went with her father, so she was separated from the other two siblings. They moved in with us at a young age, seven and nine years old. My cousins didn't have a dependable father. He was depressed and isolated himself after the divorce and gave up on life. He stopped working, moved in with his parents and smoked, took prescription drugs, and drank himself into a depression. My father and mother stepped up and adopted the kids as their own. My aunt told my father if something ever happened to her that she wanted my dad to take care of her kids.

It was hard for all of us. We had a huge change in our lives that turned everything upside down. I had to grow up fast and step up to the plate to help. I wanted to protect my siblings and my cousins from this crazy roller-coaster of a life we lived in. We lived in a thousand square foot home with two bedrooms and a garage that was turned into a room. We were all scrunched up in a very small house with no privacy so we could see all the time what was going in the home. There was nowhere to hide when times got bad with screaming matches, cussing, and abuse. We were so desperate to feel love and all we endured at the time was brokenness and fear. It's a lot for a child to experience so much pain and so many sleepless nights. We were worried death was closing in on us by the beatings of my mother, or my father getting killed in a wreck from drinking and driving.

One night my mother had a nervous breakdown. She was so drunk, depressed, and frightened by my dad she went outside in the middle of the night screaming; crying so loud and waking the neighborhood. She laid in the middle of the street on her back wanting to die. She hated her life and having to deal with my father's ups and downs and day to day behavior. She was running up and down the street and around the corner into someone else's yard. She hid behind a tree so my dad wouldn't find her. She was in fear for her life.

The pain my mom was suffering was so terrible. I remember chasing after her and trying to find her to bring her home. It was so sad to see her in so much pain. I loved my mom and I wanted to make the pain go away, but I couldn't. I was helpless. The constant agony of not knowing what was about to happen to her, or my father, was such a heavy burden for a teenager to have to handle. My mom just wanted a way out of this abusive marriage.

This happened several times throughout my childhood with my mom breaking down at night, crying in the streets while people were asleep. I had to go get her so many times after she took off and help her to calm down and come back home safely.

DEFINITION AGONY:

"Extreme physical or mental suffering. Examples: she crashed to the ground in agony" synonyms: pain, hurt, suffering, torture, torment, anguish, affliction, trauma, wretchedness; misery, distress, grief, woe, heartbreak, heartache, rare excruciation; "she was screaming in agony or the final stages of a difficult or painful death. Her last agony"[1]

This definition explains my mother's feelings exactly during these excruciating events. At the time I didn't know who Jesus really was so I didn't have the wisdom to speak life into her, but just to hold her, love on her, and tell her everything would be okay. No child should ever have to worry about being in this situation, or have to take on a parental role. Children should experience love and happiness, not dread and fear.

Husbands, love your wives and do not be harsh with them.

Colossians 3:19, NIV

You, LORD, hear the desire of the afflicted; you encourage them, and you listen to their cry, defending the fatherless and the oppressed, so that mere earthly mortals will never again strike terror.

Psalm 10:17-18, NIV

When my father wasn't drinking he was such a sweet man. He was the complete opposite person when he was sober. I was close to him and was a daddy's girl when he was normal. As I got older, I felt more hurt and betrayed by my father's actions. I remember one time my dad got so mad at me he picked me up by my neck with my feet dangling and was choking me. Another time he slammed me against one of those big televisions that used to sit on the floor and almost knocked me out. The worse he got, the more I would try to defend myself, my siblings, my cousins, and my mother. I would not back down and stood up for all of us. It didn't always go my way when this happened. I would get hurt in the middle of my father's rages.

> When you follow the desires of your sinful nature, the results are very clear: sexual immorality, impurity, lustful pleasures, idolatry, sorcery, hostility, quarreling, jealousy, outbursts of anger, selfish ambition, dissension, division, envy, drunkenness, wild parties, and other sins like these. Let me tell you again, as I have before, that anyone living that sort of life will not inherit the Kingdom of God.
>
> Galatians 5:19-21, NLT

There was a time when we went to go visit my other grandmother on my father's side, Grandma Red, and her husband. We were driving back from Hinton, OK to go back home. My father was in the car in front of us and I was in a car behind him. I remember watching my father drift off into other lanes, driving fast, swerving while he was drunk. I was so terrified. I was in complete stress and anxiety watching him drive. There were a couple close moments where he almost hit another car in the oncoming traffic. I thought right then and there my father was about to die from a terrible car accident and kill another innocent bystander from his irresponsible driving while intoxicated. I remember screaming, crying, and trying to yell for him to get back in his lane. Of course he couldn't hear me since I was in another car. I almost had a nervous breakdown.

My father had a rough childhood. His mother and father were alcoholics too. My father quit school when he was fourteen years old to take care of his sister and little brother. They were abandoned by his mother and father when his parents separated. His mom took off with another man and my father was left to be the parent and take care of his siblings. What a terrible feeling that must be to be left by your parents to take care of your brother and sister without any resources or means to provide for them.

My father and his siblings had to move in with his uncle to be looked after. My father also had to grow up very fast and didn't get to have a healthy childhood. He was neglected, abandoned, physically abused by his father, and treated poorly. My father never knew what a loving family should look like, so he had no clue how to be a parent himself. He made the same mistakes as his parents did because that was all he had known. My father was a child himself. My father had to live through this vicious cycle of abuse that ultimately carried over to his life as a young father and a husband.

My father was nineteen and my mother was twenty-six when they had me. There were times I prayed for God to touch my hand just once for me to feel Him or to reveal Himself to me. I would go outside in my backyard late at night, lay on the cement porch, and look into the sky staring at the abyss in the darkness, but saw God's beauty in the stars shining above me. That gave me reassurance even through the darkness God gave light for me to see. He wanted me to hang onto it. He was shining His love for me when I didn't understand at the time. The stars reminded me of God's sparkle in His eyes looking down on me, showing me He was there for me. But as I child I didn't know what that meant, and I didn't know who God was.

My grandma Ruth loved Jesus. She would start whispering in my ear and telling me there is a greater love out there. There is a God who created us here on earth and He loved us so much. She started to explain to me who he was but I didn't quite understand what she was telling me yet because I was still very young. She was speaking life into me so I could breathe God's love over my soul; showing me the freedom that I needed to learn so one day I would make that choice on my own to receive Christ as my Lord and Savior.

I remember being on her lap, crying hysterically that I didn't want to die. I feared death and being alone. She would give me love and reassurance that I needed to hear so I would be calm, relax, and feel peace and happiness. At the time I didn't know, but God was making me brave and molding me to be an extremely tough person that could handle all sorts of life trials that came my way. There was power in the name of Jesus speaking to my grandma to speak to me and my spirit.

As I became a teenager, I became angry, disappointed, frustrated, and especially felt neglected. The feelings grew so strong as my father was gone; I felt abandoned. When he disappeared to jail for his drinking and driving, I felt somewhat relieved because he could no longer harm others or himself. I loved my daddy and I wanted him to get well. All I wanted was to feel loved and accepted. I felt insecure and unwanted, longing for something more to feel, but I didn't know what that was.

After years of abuse my mom finally left my father because she couldn't take it any longer. She filed divorce Oct 23, 2000 and it was finalized October 16, 2001. My father got so bad when she left him that he wrote a suicide note August 10, 2001. Seventeen days later, on August 27, when he was finally getting the courage to take his own life, he decided to go out drinking and driving again. He was in a parking lot at a grocery store and hit another vehicle. This was the last straw for my father, and he got arrested and taken to jail again, and spent two years in prison this time.

While he was in jail, he accepted Jesus Christ in his heart on or around September 13, 2001. Praise Jesus. I was thrilled to read the letter that my father wrote me to tell me that exciting news. When my father was away from all substances he could abuse, he was able to think clearly and realized what all his actions cost in his life: losing his wife, his children, and his home. He hit rock bottom and lost pretty much everything he cared about. I am so thankful it took him being arrested and almost losing his life to finally give it all up and throw his hands up in the air, surrendering his life over to Jesus. When I was told this, it was the happiest moment in my life. God heard my cries and answered my prayers and saved my daddy.

Praise:

Thank you, Jesus, for loving my Grandma Ruth so much to give her wisdom of You. During the painful experiences and places in my life You gave me the wisdom as well as a healthy perspective of the right mind of thinking. Thank You for showing me the truth about life events, about myself, and seeing through other people's eyes during their tough times in life. You helped and guided me to see through Your eyes of love. You encouraged me during those hurts and frustrations in my thoughts; helpless feelings of emotion and not being in control. You gave me a new way to respond appropriately to handle difficult times in my life. I know I wasn't perfect, but You helped me to no longer punish myself inwardly or to others. You helped me through my addictive behavior to be wanted by the wrong crowds or relationships. Lord, I carried these wounds for so long in my life. It took a long time to practice but by Your help You stopped the pain within and healed me so I could enjoy living life freely. Lord, thank You for opening my eyes to see You are my constant reminder. You are my Healer and You believed in me when I didn't believe in myself. You guided me and encouraged me to face my fears even when I didn't want to confront the pain head on. Your love is like sparkles of fireworks flashing over and over in the water. It's the reflection of the sun. This is Your love telling me it is everlasting and constant; that You will never waiver. You are my beginning and my end. Thank You, my precious King, how worthy You are.

OUR PROTECTOR, GUARDIAN AND DEFENDER

A person or thing that protects someone or something. Examples: defender, preserver, bodyguard, minder, guardian, guard, champion, watchdog, ombudsman, knight in shining armor, guardian angel, patron, chaperone, escort, keeper, custodian; guard, shield, pad, buffer, cushion, protection or a person in charge of kingdom during the minority, absence, or incapacity of the sovereign.[2]

He will cover you with his feathers, and under his wings you will find refuge; his faithfulness will be your shield and rampart. You will not fear the terror of night, nor the arrow that flies by day.

Psalm 91:4-5, NIV

Even though I walk through the darkest valley, I will fear no evil, for you are with me; your rod and your staff, they comfort me.

Psalm 23:4 NIV

For he guards the course of the just and protects the way of his faithful ones.

Proverbs 2:8 NIV

He is my loving God and my fortress, my stronghold and my deliverer, my shield, in whom I take refuge, who subdues peoples under me.

Psalm 144:2, NIV

He said: "The LORD is my rock, my fortress and my deliver;"

2 Samuel 22:2, NIV

The righteous person may have many troubles, but the Lord delivers him from them all.

Psalm 34:19, NIV

I believe our Father wants us well. He wants to take away the pain from the past, and the fatigue in our bodies from experiencing hardship. Our bodies may feel beaten up with the constant blows that the devil tries to throw our way. Storms will come throughout our lives, but they reveal many truths in us to help with healing. As we continue with our battles in life, let's make a promise to ourselves to not allow them to disable our thoughts, or handicap us, but allow Christ to bring victory in our lives.

Remember to let it be, God will direct you through your down moments. He will help you recognize warnings to not allow your thoughts to hold you captive. God will speak love and reassurance over you every day. He wired those specific weaknesses in our lives to help us cry out to Him for healing. Admit to yourself with honesty where you are at in your pain so God can help you through these frustrating moments. We will be more alert when the devil starts creeping in to distract us from God. God is our Savior and we don't need to be afraid. Allow yourself to be joyful in the moment. Don't worry about when the next test is going to happen, but be joyful warriors that are grateful in moments of heartache.

> Be alert and of sober mind. Your enemy the devil prowls around like a roaring lion looking for someone to devour. Resist him, standing firm in the faith, because you know that the family of believers throughout the world is undergoing the same kind of sufferings. And the God of all grace, who called you to his eternal glory in Christ, after you have suffered a little while, will himself restore you and make you strong, firm and steadfast.
>
> 1 Peter 5:8-10, NIV

DISORDERS FROM NEGLECT

DEFINITION OF NEGLECT:
"Fail to be cared for properly, abandoned; forsaken, run down, shackled, untended, unweed, disrepair, deterioration or disuse. This is what the devil wants us to feel. However, Jesus wants us to feel this."

DEFINITION OF REVIVAL:

"An improvement in the condition or strength of something. Examples: improvement, rallying, betterment, amelioration, advance, rally, upturn, upswing, comeback, resurgence, renewal, picking up, turn for the better."

"Or an instance feeling important again. Examples comeback, re-establishment, reintroduction, restoration, reappearance, resurrections."[3]

RAD, ALSO KNOWN AS REACTIVE ATTACHMENT DISORDER

I wanted to talk about an important disorder that children can develop from neglect or abandonment. A lot of children that get taken away from their home end up in foster care. They are left alone: abandoned with no one to take care of them; abused with their parents getting taken away to jail for their crimes; neglected, causing disruption at an early age of the relationship with parents or caregivers. All of these things cause the child to have attachment issues. They were never truly able to experience a healthy bond with their parents. This causes enormous emotional issues with the developmental stage of their lives.

Most children that have experienced trauma in their lives developed a feeling of being unsafe or alone. They lose their trust for others. When their self-worth feels broken, they start acting out by dissociating themselves from others. When a child repeatedly feels isolated or uncared for in the environment they are in, it can cause the child to become extremely frightened all the time. If a child never knows what to expect from their parents it's hard to make sense of what is happening all around them. They feel their needs are not been taken care of when they are not comforted, left hungry for hours, or left in a dirty diaper for long periods at a time with no interaction. In the child's mind, what is being demonstrated to them is that no one cares for them. It can break the child's soul. They can struggle with control issues when they get older. To avoid feeling helpless they can become disobedient, defiant, and argumentative. The anger can stir up tantrums, and they can rebel, be manipulative, or passive-aggressive toward others.

This explains some of my behaviors as a child. I rebelled, lashed out with anger, always in fear what of what was going to happen to me or to my parents. I was fearful of death-that my parents would die and I would be left alone. I went through so many ups and downs with emotions. I became out of control at times with my anger toward my parents. I hated my life so much then. I felt like I was living in a constant hell; a repeated cycle of torment day after day, worrying how the next day was going to be.

I developed a broken attachment from my parents. I didn't have a connection with them. It was hard to be close with them at times from the pain they brought to our home. I loved them but was very angry at them for not nurturing me or my siblings and cousins the way a parent should. It caused resentment in my soul toward them. There were no boundaries or routines ever set for us. There was so much chaos in the home we didn't know which way to turn. There was no order. This can be very confusing to a child.

Every child should have rules, what is and is not allowed in the home. We needed limits to be set and if we didn't follow those rules, we would needed consequences for our actions. The inconsistency in the home was hard for all of us kids. Children need schedules to follow so it can help with the development stage of their life. When conflict is in the home it can cause the child to struggle emotionally. Socially a child will either isolate themselves for the fear of being rejected, or a child will be out of control, craving attention that can be harmful for them or others. Children need to learn empathy, to care for others and know the meaning of love. When this is broken, it can cause narcissistic tendencies.

NARCISSISTIC BEHAVIOR

In a child, narcissistic behavior can develop many ways. If a parent is always putting the child down or belittling them and holding unrealistic expectations that a child can't meet. If they are being told and grilled in their heads that they need to be the best at everything, by winning every game they play or having the best grades. If a child feels the pressure, can't meet the needs of their parent, or feels inadequate, humiliated, or ashamed of their actions, they can spiral down building hatred toward their parents. If the inner shame gets the best of the child, they can be impulsive and develop addictive behaviors. Examples including alcohol abuse, drug abuse, overspending habits, social media addiction, and sexual addiction.

The narcissist can become a perfectionist, striving to be the best at everything they do because what was expected of them at a young age. If they don't achieve what is expected of them, then they feel unloved or unwanted by the parent. In order to feel that love from their parent they start developing a constant need to prove their self-worth by trying to be the best and not disappoint their parent. The more they try to achieve unrealistic accomplishments for their parents they get used to wanting the constant praise, admiration, and worship of others when they compliment their greatness.

If a child continues to be harassed by their parent saying they're not good enough, they can develop a hatred that can be so toxic that anyone who is in their way will become the target for the hatred that is building inside of them. As the child gets older, psychopathic tendencies can stir up inside of them by the need to feed the feeling of their ego with danger or the pleasure of their sickly addictions.

EXAMPLES OF NARCISSISTIC BEHAVIOR:

1) NO EMPATHY

These people truly don't have the capacity for empathy. They do not have the ability to authentically embrace the experiential world of another person unless it is for self-ish gain. In other words, these people can put on a good "caring" show in their effort to manipulate others for their own personal benefit. But they won't, and can't, stand in the shoes of another, genuinely.

2) NO REMORSE

These people don't feel bad about any wrongdoing. Why? There is no conscience, no compassion, no concern about the impact of their behavior on others, even those they love. From the narcissistic abuser's point of view, the other person deserves what they got because the narcissistic abuser is...

3) ENTITLED

These people hold rights—in their perverted thinking—that others would never assume. They live in a world in which they have privilege to that which is beyond your imagination. Whether they are objectifying you, raping you, or ruling your life, they believe that they deserve what they seek, when and where they seek it because it is already theirs—they don't have to ask.

4) DECEPTIVE

They will tell you whatever they believe you need to know in order to get what they are attempting to extract from you. To these people, a lie is not a lie; it's a mechanism to leverage outcome. A misrepresentation of information is the twisting of facts designed to convert another into compliance with respect to that which they pursue.

5) DR. JEKYLL/MR. HYDE

These people will project a persona that is 180 degrees from who and what they really are. Whether priest, doctor, or politician, they are not as they wish to have you believe. For example, they can be an attorney allegedly protecting an elderly woman from financial exploitation; all while emotionally manipulating/exploiting her, by using her in a mission to influence.

6) EMOTIONALLY DEPENDENT

These people require the emotional support and admiration of their narcissistic supply as much as oxygen to sustain them. They truly cannot function naturally and normally without the object of their narcissistic abuse serving as the foundation for their existence.

7) USES BATTERING FOR CONTROL

And when their narcissistic supply is in question, battering becomes the way to level the playing field. It is their means to shift the power and control within the relationship. It's their way to tip the scale, so they gain the advantage they need to feel on top again.

> This battering may present as verbal abuse, emotional abuse, financial abuse, sexual abuse, or physical abuse. It's the striking/maneuvering intended to diminish and dis-empower so as to nourish the deficiency in oneself.
>
> DR. JEANNE KING, PH.D.[4]

BIPOLAR DISORDER

This is a serious condition that has impulsive and self-destructive behavior. Having this disorder can cause overwhelming thoughts of suicide. Their behavior is reckless. They can make foolish investments, go on shopping sprees, or take impulsive sexual risks that can be out of control when they are in a manic and hypomanic episode. The mental health condition of the person can affect the mood and energy levels in the body. When the symptoms get worse, the person can become in a manic state of severe hopelessness and extreme irritability, distractibility, and irregular sleep patterns. There are contributing factors that cause this disorder such as genetics, stress, traumatic event that occurred in their life, drug or alcohol abuse, and hormonal imbalance.

If you don't get help with this condition the complications can get worse and affect the home by damaging relationships, cheating on a spouse, running away from home, performing poorly at work or in school, and struggling with financial problems. It can even end with death by suicide. Some people who have bipolar disorder also have other disorders. They could have anxiety, ADHD, physical health problems, or eating disorders. The list can go on. Please make sure you pay attention to the warning signs of your body or a loved one around you. Identify the patterns or triggers that keep creeping up in you or your loved one so you can try to get help when an episode occurs. You will be better equipped for handling it when it comes.

COMMON SYMPTOMS OF BIPOLAR
    "MANIA: THE "HIGHS" OF BIPOLAR DISORDER
    Symptoms of mania include

- heightened mood, exaggerated optimism and self-confidence;
- excessive irritability, aggressive behavior;
- decreased need for sleep without experiencing fatigue;
- grandiose thoughts, inflated sense of self-importance;
- racing speech, racing thoughts, flight of ideas;
- impulsiveness, poor judgment, easily distracted;
- reckless behavior; and
- in the most severe cases, delusions and hallucinations.

DEPRESSION: THE "LOWS" OF BIPOLAR DISORDER

Symptoms of depression include

- prolonged sadness or unexplained crying spells;
- significant changes in appetite and sleep patterns;
- irritability, anger, worry, agitation, anxiety;
- pessimism, indifference;
- loss of energy, persistent lethargy;
- feelings of guilt, worthlessness;
- inability to concentrate, indecisiveness;
- inability to take pleasure in former interests, social withdrawal;
- unexplained aches and pains; and
- recurring thoughts of death or suicide.[5]

My point in explaining these disorders is to help you recognize what is going on with you or others in your life. The importance of being a parent and the role we have to our children is by teaching them a good example of what a healthy family should look like so they don't develop wrong behaviors. If we can avoid this happening to our children, we can help our children to succeed developmentally in the right way. I don't want to discourage anyone by saying that you are doing something wrong. I want you to be aware of the little ones that are watching our every move. We are the ones they see every day and look to for guidance. We are their role models so we must be conscious of how we represent ourselves around others to protect the innocence ones.

If you are experiencing any of these disorders from your past hurts, I would seek help to understand what you are feeling so you can learn the skills to cope with these emotions to protect yourself and others surrounding you. It's better to be aware of what you are experiencing so you can help others that are in need the same way you needed help. It's okay to be vulnerable and ask for help when it's needed. Believe me, I have had many years of counseling to sort through my emotions and to recognize what was happening to my body.

Some people may have a chemical imbalance with the serotonin produced by nerve cells in the brain where they may need extra help by taking anti-depressants. Don't be ashamed to use this if this is something that can help you out. It can help regulate the dopamine that is a chemical messenger in the brain, called neurotransmitters, and the mood that may be off in the body. I have been on this to help me out to regulate my body. For the longest time I was ashamed and didn't want people know I had been taking anti-depressants, but this truly has helped me get regulated when I am going through highs and lows with my emotions. This has allowed me to balance my body correctly to avoid irritable mood swings, sadness, and anxiety.

There may be difficult days that will continue to come even with medicine, but what you do during those difficult times is keep pushing forward when the pain hurts. Use the resources you learned to better equip yourself to cope when these feelings arise out of nowhere. They can sneak up out of the blue. When we have these skills and Christ with us, we can get through all the powerful emotions that come to attack. The frustration tries to come headstrong. This is when to fight and let God's army work for you. The angels are in a war fighting the demons that come your way that we cannot see. The demons' mission is to get you off course from God's will for your life.

Prayer:

I pray Jesus for all the hurting people out there. Help them to recognize what is happening to their bodies. Teach them to learn a great deal about themselves. I pray that they will find the way to break the feeling of hopelessness and loss of self-control. Help them to lay down all their worries of pain or defeat from the disorders they are experiencing. Heal them inside and out. Give them strength to believe in themselves and gain confidence. Help them to learn to react to the problem by seeking help the way they feel when episodes appear, whether that is counseling, medication, meditation, or prayer. Let them not feel ashamed but know they will be used for Your good. In Your precious name, Amen.

He who gains wisdom *and* good sense loves (preserves) his own soul; He who keeps understanding will find good *and* prosper.

Proverbs 19:8, AMP

3

Sexual Abuse

But if the man meets the engaged woman out in the country, and he rapes her, then only the man must die. Do nothing to the young woman; she has committed no crime worthy of death. She is as innocent as a murder victim. Since the man raped her out in the country, it must be assumed that she screamed, but there was no one to rescue her.

Deuteronomy 22:25-27, NLT

Here is the perspective of an innocent child around five years old visiting her grandparents one sunny morning. It seemed like any other day when I was visiting them. They would make us pancakes for breakfast. My grandma loved putting tomato soup on the pancakes, along with my mother and older sister, which seemed a little strange to me but hey if they liked it that way good for them. I myself liked peanut butter and syrup on top. I know you are probably thinking, *what a weird family they are*, but I enjoyed those moments with them. They were always dear to my heart.

Usually for lunchtime my grandma would love making us peanut butter and jelly sandwiches. She'd mix the jelly and peanut butter together in a bowl, then she would put it on the bread and cut it in half for me and my little brother. The way my grandma made it was her special love she put in it that tasted yummier than my parents would make us. I looked up to my grandparents, especially my sweet and loving Grandma Ruth. After lunch one day my grandma left, and I stayed with my grandpa. I don't recall the reason at the time why she left but she was not there with me.

I was helping them clean their home. I was cleaning the front glass door and I was standing on a ladder. My grandfather asked me if I like to have sex. I said yes. However, I didn't have a clue what that word meant, nor did I really understand the question he was asking me. He was watching me clean the door and I am not sure what his thoughts were at that moment. I don't know why he got the urge to ask me that question.

He took me into his room which seemed a little weird to me, but not too much because I would go in my grandparents' room a lot to watch tv in there. They had two separate twin-sized beds. I would usually lay on my grandma's side to watch cartoons or play dress up with her jewelry.

I know I felt ashamed but didn't know why. I was molested by my grandpa, my mother's father. I was five years old and very confused about what had happened to me. I never spoke about what happened to my mother. I went home with mom and felt betrayed by my grandpa for taking advantage of me. In a five-year-old there are too many emotions that go on in their minds. I didn't understand the meaning of my feelings or what had happened.

Another time when I went to visit my grandparents again my grandpa took me in his truck away from his home to try to do the same thing to me. My grandma was at the house and he took me to do an errand to have an excuse to do the same thing to me. I don't know how long this episode lasted but whatever he was doing he got enough of the pleasure he needed at that time to finally stop doing what he was doing to me. When we got back, I still didn't speak of what happened to me.

The last time he ever tried to touch me again he took me in the backyard where there was a shed to do dirty things to me. I remember my mom and grandma calling my name looking for me. My grandpa told me to hush so he wouldn't get caught with me in the shed. I screamed when I was in the shed and came out running and they saw my grandfather coming out of the shed. I was so scared. I told my mother what was going on and what her father was doing to me. My mom was furious and took me home. At first my grandma didn't believe me because she didn't want to know that her husband was a pedophile that liked to be with little girls. She was a Christian woman of strong faith, but her faith was tested when she found out what her husband was doing to me. I never went over to their house again. My parents kept me away from there. That was the last time I remember being with him.

My father's sister was married to my mom's brother. They had kids together. They would bring my cousins to visit my grandparents. My aunt and uncle split up so the two little kids would go over to my grandparents a lot when their dad moved in with my grandparents. My aunt's best friend turned my aunt and uncle into DHS. From what I understand, she saw signs that my little cousin seemed to be abused. She was worried something terrible happened to my little cousin. I don't recall exactly how this happened, but my cousin was taken away from my aunt and uncle because they saw things on my cousin that indicated that she was being molested when she was examined. She was taken by DHS and placed in foster care. He started trying to molest my cousin who was around one to two years old. She was a little innocent baby that had no clue about life. She was a sweet little girl. A baby shouldn't ever have to experience such a horrendous abuse.

When you love someone so dearly and they do this to you, you don't understand what you did wrong or why they would want to touch you like that. My grandpa was an addict with prescription pills. He took lots of them and was heavily medicated. I don't know if he had mental issues, or if this even happened to him as a child, but that is not an excuse to do that to an innocent child, or betray his wife by doing something that was evil and cruel.

My grandma was a strong believer in Christ. She loved God and it was very important to her to live her life right and be the best she could be. She was a very strict parent. She would be there for her kids and try to keep them from making poor decisions as a teenager. They all went to church together. My grandmother cleaned homes and my grandfather worked at a flour mill in a factory. If someone was looking in, it would seem like any normal family.

However, my grandfather had a hidden secret–liking children and being attracted to underage kids. My grandma never knew she was married to a pedophile. The sad part was, my grandmother was also molested by her dad. Her dad was sick in his head and abusive. He would make my grandma and her other siblings sleep in the same bed with him. He fondled and molested them for many years of their life. This was a curse in our family history that had a major effect of being a pedophile or allowing sex to drive their minds to unhealthy thoughts and actions. My grandma's dad ended up going into a mental facility for pedophilia and being mentally unstable. He was never released and died in there of a heart attack.

There was a cousin in our family that I never met. He died before I was born by taking his own life. He was the cousin of my mom's dad and was very sick in his head too. He was thrown in jail for molesting his own kids, and tried to do the same to my mother's sister one night when he was taking her home. She was able to fight him off so luckily she didn't have to experience that type of pain and abuse. She was still traumatized by the event that did occur.

My mother finally admitted to me that her father tried to do the same thing to me, but she was able to stop him from abusing her. My mother told me that my grandma's dad molested her at a young age, around five as well. When this happened, my mother was never the same again. She was always a scared little girl who had panic attacks, and was always frightened that someone was going to hurt her. She developed depression, insecurity and anxiety. She was unable to focus and became very nervous all the time.

It finally took a toll on my mother and she lost control. She started to rebel at home and started to party. She just wanted to get out of her parents' house. She got married when she was seventeen and had my sister when she was eighteen. Her husband was very abusive to her so my mother wanted out of the marriage. He told her if she wouldn't let my sister go with him that he would kill her, so my mother, in fear of her life, gave in and let her daughter live with her father so they could get divorced.

Later in life my mother was put on anti-depressants and has been on them ever since. She has gone to so much counseling because of the abuse. She had to talk to someone to get help from all the ups and downs she was feeling. She was always taught to keep things to herself and not let others know what happened to her in life. It took her many years of counseling, but she finally felt that she could move on from these devasting events. She said she will never forget what happened to her, but she has learned how to manage it in her life. She doesn't let it affect her any longer. She has dealt with the pain.

"When the Spirit of truth comes, he will guide you into all truth. He will not speak on his own but will tell you what he has heard. He will tell you about the future."

John 16:13, NLT

The LORD is close to the brokenhearted; he rescues those whose spirits are crushed.

Psalm 34:18, NLT

"BETRAYAL"

THE RAPE OF TAMAR

Now David's son Absalom had a beautiful sister named Tamar. And Amnon, her half brother, fell desperately in love with her. Amnon became so obsessed with Tamar that he became ill. She was a virgin, and Amnon thought he could never have her.

But Amnon had a very crafty friend—his cousin Jonadab. He was the son of David's brother Shimea. One day Jonadab said to Amnon, "What's the trouble? Why should the son of a king look so dejected morning after morning?"

So Amnon told him, "I am in love with Tamar, my brother Absalom's sister."

"Well," Jonadab said, "I'll tell you what to do. Go back to bed and pretend you are ill. When your father comes to see you, ask him to let Tamar come and prepare some food for you. Tell him you'll feel better if she prepares it as you watch and feeds you with her own hands."

So Amnon lay down and pretended to be sick. And when the king came to see him, Amnon asked him, "Please let my sister Tamar come and cook my favorite dish as I watch. Then I can eat it from her own hands." So David agreed and sent Tamar to Amnon's house to prepare some food for him.

When Tamar arrived at Amnon's house, she went to the place where he was lying down so he could watch her mix some dough. Then she baked his favorite dish for him. But when she set the serving tray before him, he refused to eat. "Everyone get out of here," Amnon told his servants. So they all left.

Then he said to Tamar, "Now bring the food into my bedroom and feed it to me here." So Tamar took his favorite dish to him. But as she was feeding him, he grabbed her and demanded, "Come to bed with me, my darling sister."

"No, my brother!" she cried. "Don't be foolish! Don't do this to me! Such wicked things aren't done in Israel. Where could I go in my shame? And you would be called one of the greatest fools in Israel. Please, just speak to the king about it, and he will let you marry me."

But Amnon wouldn't listen to her, and since he was stronger than she was, he raped her. Then suddenly Amnon's love turned to hate, and he hated her even more than he had loved her. "Get out of here!" he snarled at her.

"No, no!" Tamar cried. "Sending me away now is worse than what you've already done to me."

But Amnon wouldn't listen to her. He shouted for his servant and demanded, "Throw this woman out, and lock the door behind her!"

So the servant put her out and locked the door behind her. She was wearing a long, beautiful robe, as was the custom in those days for the king's virgin daughters. But now Tamar tore her robe and put ashes on her head. And then, with her face in her hands, she went away crying.

Her brother Absalom saw her and asked, "Is it true that Amnon has been with you? Well, my sister, keep quiet for now, since he's your brother. Don't you worry about it." So Tamar lived as a desolate woman in her brother Absalom's house.

When King David heard what had happened, he was very angry.

2 Sam 13:1-21 NLT

Why didn't David punish Amnon for his sin against Tamar? Many reasons have been suggested. One likely reason is that Amnon was David's son, and that David had been guilty of sexual sin himself (in the case of Bathsheba)—therefore, in the case of Amnon and Tamar, he felt inadequate to judge. Another possible reason is that there were no witnesses to the crime. Amnon's friend Jonadab had carefully orchestrated the crime to avoid the possibility of witnesses;

therefore, there was no way to prove the crime according to Jewish law.

Regardless of the reason, Absalom took matters into his own hands. He avenged Tamar by killing their half-brother Amnon, though it resulted in many problems for himself. Absalom lived away from his family for three years after the murder, and then lived for an additional period in Jerusalem before again seeing his father's face. Absalom would also later seek to usurp his father's throne, resulting in his own death.

The wretched, tragic story of Amnon and Tamar highlights some of the problems associated with sexual sin and its aftermath. No one should experience the treatment Tamar endured, and it is important to respond to such situations with integrity and justice. David neglected justice, and Absalom implemented his own standards, creating additional problems in the process.[6]

Have you ever felt alone, ashamed, suicidal, resentful of what has happened to you? Molestation and rape are very serious crimes. No one should ever have to endure such betrayal. There have been many children, boys and girls, women and men, that have experienced abuse from a loved one or someone close to them. I am speaking from experience. The pain and damage that does to a person is indescribable. The pain you have experienced may have left you feeling undesirable, unwanted or damaged. We may feel like no one would ever truly love us if they found out what had happened, but this is simply not true. God loves us more than words can describe.

We may feel rotten in our bones. What happens to you in life is not as important as the choices you make from the outcome of the incident. Do you ever ask yourself, *what is wrong with me? Why would someone want to do this to me? Did I give them the wrong attention or signals for that person to want to commit a horrific crime against me? Why me Lord?*

We can go on and on asking questions to try to figure out the meaning of what happened to us. Don't let yourself be the victim. Let's be victorious in Christ. Let's not ponder over our shortcomings, or the mess we feel inside. We can be our own worst enemies. The devil tries to use us as a pawn to try to get to Jesus by showing Him we were damaged in the beginning when we were created. The reality is, we can be a magnet of insecurity by the lies that Satan tries to threaten us with-that we are worthless or forgotten. Don't make a harsh assessment of yourself, but let Jesus show you what he sees in you. We lack no good thing. The enemy has no claim on us.

Don't miss true happiness or joy because you are so focused or caught up by your failures of self-contempt. We are God's masterpieces. Jesus made us perfect just the way we are and made us holy through His loving hands. He is committed to us to restore our souls.

What will it take for you to be comfortable in your own skin?

For we are God's masterpiece. He has created us anew in Christ Jesus, so we can do the good things he planned for us long ago.

Eph 2:10, NLT

This is real love—not that we loved God, but that he loved us and sent his Son as a sacrifice to take away our sins.

1 John 4:10, NLT

You must wake up with a conscious decision every day that you are loved by God. His grace and truth declare us free from the enemy's hands. Satan is a true parasite in your life.

DICTIONARY DEFINITION OF PARASITE

"A follower who hangs around a host (without benefit to the host) in hope of gain or advantage. Examples leech or sponge. The type of follower is a person who accepts the leadership of another."

This is exactly what Satan is to us. He tries to take over our body by making us feel weak or vulnerable with no return, so he can creep in and destroy us from the inside out. He tries to torment us until we can no longer function so that we would want to destroy ourselves by making terrible decisions to harm our bodies with sex, drugs, and alcohol; or bodily harm by cutting, burning ourselves, or depriving our body by starvation, or taking our own life. Satan is an unwanted invader that tries to make a habitat in our minds, or make residence in our every thought process to destroy our soul or home.

God doesn't fear our messes. He is moved by them. He wants to demonstrate his love through us and inside our souls. Don't get complacent here on earth through pain. Let's take away the devil's ability to take power over our lives and remind ourselves that Jesus loves us through our dark moments. He doesn't give up on us. He wants to rejoice in everything that we experience through sadness to joy. God will use our story as a weapon and turn it against Satan.

> "Afflicted city, storm-battered, unpitied:
>   I'm about to rebuild you with stones of turquoise,
> Lay your foundations with sapphires,
>   construct your towers with rubies,
> Your gates with jewels,
>   and all your walls with precious stones.
> All your children will have God for their teacher—
>   what a mentor for your children!
> You'll be built solid, grounded in righteousness,
>   far from any trouble—nothing to fear!
>   far from terror—it won't even come close!
> If anyone attacks you,
>   don't for a moment suppose that I sent them,
> And if any should attack,
>   nothing will come of it.
> I create the blacksmith

who fires up his forge

and makes a weapon designed to kill.

I also create the destroyer—

but no weapon that can hurt you has ever been forged.

Any accuser who takes you to court

will be dismissed as a liar.

This is what God's servants can expect.

I'll see to it that everything works out for the best."

God's Decree.

Isaiah 54:11-17, MSG

God is the keeper of our hearts. He restores our souls in the wilderness season. The only hindrance is us. What happens in our souls, happens to ourselves. God will restore our souls. Don't let the fear get to you. God will always be with you. God will not let us lose. God is here to fight with you and stomp the devil's head down.

Praise:

Thank You, God, that we are not who we were, or what we have done. Thank You for loving us so much that You always see the true self during our pain. Thank You for reaching out and grabbing a hold of our hands to pull us out of the pit of despair. Thank You for what we have gone through so we can believe that we are healed through Jesus' resurrection and nailing every pain on the cross and allowing our hearts to acknowledge our past hurts so we can have the freedom of joy and the breakthrough of our pain. We feast on your determined purpose in our lives to bring miracles by preparing and promoting our spirits while

You work on our souls and fight our battles for us when we are at our weakest moments.

Everyone please clear your minds, be still, and know that God is going to bring justice to our perpetrators who came in and violated us, causing pain in our hearts. Meditate only on God, sink down, relax and be quiet while God does His work in our lives and fights off the enemy so we can remind our spirits to let God's light shine upon our hearts.

4

Addictions

I give you all the credit, GOD—you got me out of that
mess, you didn't let my foes gloat. GOD, my God, I
yelled for help and you put me together. GOD, you
pulled me out of the grave, gave me another chance
at life when I was down-and-out.

Psalm 30:1-3, MSG

An addiction is a terrible disease to have. It can control every
part of your life. It consumes your every waking thought. The
only thing you can think about is the addiction you are craving. We all have different types of addictions such as substance
abuse, sex, overeating, seeking the wrong kind of attention
from men or women, harming yourself, hurting/violating others, excessive exercise, obsessing over the way you look, shopping, gambling, and so much more that is out there taking over
the world.

People hold themselves to a higher standard. They don't feel
like they are good enough and eventually it takes a toll on them
and they crave the wrong type of satisfaction to fulfill their
needs/wants that are missing from their lives. Most people

feel empty, deprived, or incomplete that the desperation to find something out there to feed the starvation of emptiness in their soul. The desire to feel something inside of us weighs so heavily that we become demolished into nothingness. Most people need that instant gratification to make them feel alive, or happy for that moment, but when that subsides the addiction gets greater and it's harder to maintain that high. Whatever the addiction is that you feed in your life, it can corrupt every healthy thought in your mind where eventually it takes over. The power of the addiction becomes them.

We can become unstable or offensive when someone tries to interfere with that addiction. When this happens often the individual will feel out of control and become violent if they feel backed into a corner; restrained or held down by their own free will. This too can lead them down a path of destruction if they feel someone is trying to double-cross them. The withdrawals from their addictions can have negative effects. In fact, being restricted/deprived of the ruthless addiction can lead to harm if trying to intervene. The strong desires they are grappling with overtake over sensors in their brains that have been compromised.

This really explains the scientifically what addiction does to many people's lives.

NEUROLOGICAL EFFECTS

All addictive drugs act in the brain to produce their euphoric effects. However, some can also cause damage due to seizures, stroke, and direct toxic effects on brain cells. Drug use can also lead to addiction, a brain disorder that occurs when repeated drug use leads to changes in the function of multiple brain circuits that control pleasures/reward, stress, decision-making, impulse control, learning and memory, and other functions. These changes make it harder for those with an addiction to experience pleasure in response to natural rewards—such as food, sex, or positive social interactions—or to manage their stress, control their impulses, and make the healthy choice to stop drug seeking and use.[7]

This is another really good read that explains our brains when the addiction takes a hold. I am very fascinated by how the brain works, what triggers our responses when we feed our body with all kinds of addictive behaviors. I am so curious what took my father as prisoner in his own body and why is it so hard to stop addiction. This makes a lot of sense what this does to our brain when we feed it wrong, causing triggers in the brain.

ADDICTIVE SUBSTANCES AND CHANGES IN THE BRAIN

Once someone develops an addiction, his or her brain is essentially rewired to use drugs despite the consequences. While physical symptoms of an addiction will go away, situations or emotions related to past substance abuse can trigger cravings years down the road.

This doesn't mean recovery isn't possible. But people in recovery must realize treatment is an ongoing process. Addiction treatment is developing every day and has rapidly improved over the years. If you or someone you care about is struggling to overcome an addiction, get help now.

HOW ADDICTIONS DEVELOP

The human brain is a complex organ controlling every voluntary and involuntary action we make. The brain controls basic motor skills, heart and breathing rates, emotions, behavior and decision-making.

There is a part of the brain responsible for addiction. The name for this part of the brain is the limbic system. This system, also known as the "brain reward system," is responsible for producing feelings of pleasure.

When a person takes an addictive substance, the limbic system releases chemicals that make the user feel good. This encourages habitual substance abuse. The overwhelming, involuntary need to use a substance — regardless of the harm it may cause — is due to actual changes that have occurred in the brain reward system. Feeding the addiction becomes priority number one.

ACTIVATING THE BRAIN REWARD SYSTEM

The abuse of addictive substances activates the brain reward system. Frequently activating this system with drugs can lead to addiction. The brain reward system is naturally activated when we take part in actions that are good for us. It is part of our natural ability to adapt and survive. Whenever something activates this system, the brain assumes something necessary to survival is happening. The brain then rewards that behavior by creating feelings of pleasure.

Drinking water when we are thirsty, for example, activates the reward system, so we repeat this behavior. Addictive substances hijack this system, causing feelings of pleasure for actions that are actually harmful. Unfortunately, addictive substances have a far stronger effect on the brain reward system.

THE BIOCHEMISTRY OF ADDICTION

Dopamine plays an important role in the reward system. Dopamine is a natural chemical in the brain that sends signals to the limbic system. When introduced into the limbic system, drugs either mimic dopamine or cause an overproduction of it in the brain. The reason normal actions that activate the brain reward system (food, drinking, sex, music, etc.) don't reprogram the brain for addiction is because they produce normal levels of dopamine.

Addictive substances can release up to 10 times more dopamine than natural reward behaviors.

Substance use floods neuroreceptors with dopamine. This causes the "high" associated with using drugs. After continued drug abuse, the human brain is unable to naturally produce normal levels of dopamine. In essence, drugs take the reward system hostage.

The result is craving the drugs that will restore dopamine levels to normal. A person in this scenario is no longer capable of feeling good without the drug.[8]

GENERATIONAL EFFECTS

I have a younger sister who is twenty-five years old. She has four children. She had her first child at the age of seventeen, two months away from being eighteen years old. My sweet sister has struggled so much throughout her life. She made a bad choice being with a person who was abusive to her. They were together off and on for almost ten years. This is the only true relationship she has known. From the beginning of their relationship it was unhealthy. They were young and made poor decisions along the way. From the outside looking in, she craved being wanted and loved. At a young age of her life she saw abuse right in front of her eyes. This is the only normalcy she was used to seeing every day, from infancy to age seven, when our parents got divorced.

My baby sister was only one year old when my father got arrested for a DUI, and he was sentenced to prison when she was two years old. My mother got pregnant with my little brother right before my father got arrested. He spent a year incarcerated. He got released four months after my little brother was born. Our father got in trouble again when my sister was eight years old and my little brother was six, when my parents had been divorced for only nine months after he spiraled out of control when my mom left him. My father really wasn't around when my siblings were young, so neither of them ever really had a father connection. This bond was broken at a young age of their lives.

Back to my sister's story...her ex-boyfriend was a bad influence on her. He introduced drugs to her and got her addicted. Her ex sold drugs out of their apartment where the two kids were living. He was reckless putting his kid in danger, letting felons and drug dealers come and go out of the apartment. One night they got robbed in the middle of the night when they were all sleeping, and he got pistol whipped in the face. It was very frightening for their whole family. They called the police to let them know what happened. I think that event caused suspicion to the police officers, so they began surveillance on their apartment. They saw what was going on in their apartment, so the police busted in their door while two of the youngest kids were in the home.

My sister's ex got arrested, then later released by cooperating with the police and turning into an informant to lead the officers to a higher chain of distributors. He still had to face charges for the crime he committed and pay his fines. He was ordered to appear in court, but he didn't show up to court, violating his court order and resulting in a warrant for his arrest for distribution to sell drugs. Later when he got caught, he spent a year in jail for his crime. Right before he went to jail my sister end up getting pregnant again with their third child.

My sister fell off the deep end. She moved in with my mother and brother, along with her two other kids while her boyfriend was serving time for selling drugs. My sister got worse and got connected to another person in her life who was doing meth and heroin. She started to do both drugs while she was pregnant. All along she was sneaking around in my mother's house doing this when my mom was gone or in bed. She got so addicted she stole my mother's debit card and was using it for Uber drives to get a fix for her addiction. She spent thousands of dollars on this along with collect calls to the jail to talk with her boyfriend.

My mother didn't realize what was going on because she was still mourning the loss of her husband, but my brother started to notice things were missing and he couldn't find some of the electronics in the home. My sister and her user of a friend stole them and pawned them for drugs. My brother told me what was happening. I couldn't take it anymore, so I reported her to DHS and called the cops on my sister. The two children got taken away from her and she had to spend time in jail. I was grateful then that she wasn't harming herself, her kids, or the innocent baby was inside of her. She was polluting herself with all the drugs and I was so afraid the baby was going to be harmed. I prayed and was convicted because she was my sister, but what she was doing was not okay. I felt like I needed to use tough love on her to force her to get help.

When the two kids were taken away by DHS, I felt so terrible for turning her in, but I wanted the children to be in a loving and safe home where they wouldn't be exposed to drugs. I don't know what the children were exposed to when she was doing drugs. We tried to find family members to take the children, but things kept falling through. Eventually, they were placed in custody with foster care parents. They went through several families until my sister's boyfriend's cousin was able to take the two children so they could stay together. This was hard for the children. They were innocent and didn't deserve to be in this position, separated from both of their parents. However, this was necessary in order for recovery from the drugs to begin.

This isn't the end of her story. She had her third baby while she was still in the hospital the person that she was doing drugs with brought drugs to the hospital and she did them there right after she delivered her child. This is how badly she was addicted to the drugs. DHS was coming into the hospital to place the baby to another home. I had to convince my sister to let her newborn baby be placed with my husband's brother and his wife. They cannot have children and already had two adopted children. They wanted a baby girl for so long and hadn't had an opportunity to adopt one. It's a long process to be able to adopt children. This was the chance for them. Before I presented this opportunity to my husband's brother, we prayed about it, and had to make sure my sister was 100% on board before I got their hopes up. My sister was back and forth, then finally agreed since the child would stay in the family. I explained to her they were fantastic Christians who loved Jesus. The baby would be cared for as if she was their own. They have a home filled with love, support from others, and a safe environment. They were responsible and had good jobs. Once she agreed, we presented this to them without any hesitation and knowing the risks that this child could possibly be placed back with my sister. They said yes and were very excited. All parties agreed and the baby went with my in-laws.

After my sister was released out of the hospital, she went to my mother's home where again she and her user friend were doing drugs. My brother called me. I was so furious. I had to make a firm decision to fully be all-in with the actions I was about to take. It would hurt a lot of people in the process, but I called the cops on her again and told the whereabouts of her location at my mother's home. My brother answered the door and let them into the home. They searched her room for evidence of drugs. They found some drugs. The male took the blame that it was his and he and my sister got arrested. She spent more time in jail, but less than a month. This was the last straw and she finally wanted to get clean. She had to hit rock bottom to truly want to make a change.

Later, after my sister agreed to get help, and my sister's boyfriend was released, they both were determined to get their children back. They were getting drug tested every week and had countless hours of parenting classes to attend. They both got jobs and stayed clean aside from one time her boyfriend didn't pass a test. This was a long road they were on. Shortly after her boyfriend was released, my sister got pregnant again with her fourth child. They wanted to do right with this child to count the wrongs they were doing. Everything was going well. She had her child and DHS let the baby stay with them but when a visit occurred with their oldest two girls there was an altercation where they were fighting in front of the children. One of the children told DHS what happened and they came in and took the other baby. At least she was placed with the other two girls at the father's cousin's house. All three children were together.

My sister was so upset. Finally, she and her boyfriend broke up. They realized they were not good together and made poor decisions for ten years. My sister moved back into my mothers' home. She has continued to stay clean. My sister finally agreed to let my husband's brother and wife adopt their third child she had. It was not finalized yet, but she and the father signed the paperwork to release their rights as the parents and set the motion to allow the parents to adopt the child. My mother has been there for her and re-assured her she did the right thing. She hasn't been a part of her life for two years and they had been the parents to her. They had taken care of the child since the beginning. They were so frightened they were going to lose her. As of October 11, 2019, we got a call that the adoption was complete.

My sister made a responsible decision to do what was right for the child. She will still be a part of the child's life. They have an open adoption so she can still see her child and be a part of her life. She will always be her mother. She hasn't abandoned her, but she took the necessary steps for her child to have the best life she can have and be fully loved and cared for in a safe home. God does work in miraculous ways. It may not always seem this way, especially for my sister, but now she can grow, learn, and mature, free from drugs, free from unhealthy relationship and find her way back to Jesus. And she can develop a new bond with our mother that they both need.

Prayer:

I pray for the love of my mother that she can help my sister to remember who God is, listen to His words and warning signs. Break the shackle that was holding her tight so she can run into Your arms, Jesus, to become closer to You than she could ever imagine. Use her story to help others in pain. I pray for wisdom for her life where she can recognize and avoid the wrong turn on a bumpy road. Keep her from stumbling back into the darkness. Help her to remember to be strong and stand her ground by digging her heals in firmly with a strong foothold. Teach her Oh Lord, guide her with Your love and help to make the right decisions from now on. Help her to believe in herself and to not worry that You are there for her, holding her hand. Help her to forgive herself and the sadness she feels inside. Release her broken heart.

My son, pay attention to my words and be willing to learn; Open your ears to my sayings. Do not let them escape from your sight; Keep them in the center of your heart. For they are life to those who find them, And healing and health to all their flesh. Watch over your heart with all diligence, For from it flow the springs of life. Put away from you a deceitful (lying, misleading) mouth, And put devious lips far from you. Let your eyes look directly ahead [toward the path of moral courage] And let your gaze be fixed straight in front of you [toward the path of integrity]. Consider well and watch carefully the path of your feet, And all your ways will be steadfast and sure. Do not turn away to the right nor to the left [where evil may lurk]; Turn your foot from [the path of] evil.

Proverbs 4:20-27, AMP

The reason I am sharing her story with you, is as parents we need to be cognizant of our actions. Anything negative we do causes a ripple effect that can bring insecurities out in our children. I included an important article of a father and daughter relationship that is a good tool to explain the importance of being a father. What I explained above about my sister caused a downward spiral in her life due to lack of love and safety from our father. She was acting out the way she saw our daddy do with the poor decisions he made. She found a man who represented similarities in our father. This was not a conscious decision, but she was replicating the events in her life of the only behavior she had seen. I love my sissy very much. I believe God will call her to a higher purpose in her life. Soon he will reveal His will for her. Help her to be patient while God works miracles in her life.

The Importance of the Father-Daughter Relationship

"You've probably heard that having a strong male influence is important in a young boy's life, but it's equally important for daughters to have one as well. A positive father-daughter relationship can have a huge impact on a young girl's life and even determine whether or not she develops into a strong, confident woman.

A father's influence in his daughter's life shapes her self-esteem, self-image, confidence and opinions of men.

"How Dad approaches life will serve as an example for his daughter to build off of in her own life, even if she chooses a different view of the world," says Michael Austin, associate professor of philosophy at Eastern Kentucky University and editor of Fatherhood-Philosophy for Everyone: The Dao of Daddy.

"What matters in the father-daughter relationship is that Dad seeks to live a life of integrity and honesty, avoiding hypocrisy and admitting his own shortcomings so that she has a realistic and positive example of how to deal with the world. He should try to model a reflective approach to life's big questions so that she can seek to do the same," he adds.

Dads and daughters: From infant to toddler

We now live in a culture where Dad is an equal partner in care giving. From day one, dads are encouraged to be hands-on, changing diapers, giving baths, putting Baby to sleep and calming her cries. That presence and effort is the beginning of a very important relationship.

According to Austin, this quality time together is crucial at all stages of a girl's life.

"Dads need to spend time with their infant daughter, taking care of her physical needs and supporting her Mom," he explains. And once the little lady starts toddling around, "[i]t's essential that Dad gets down on the floor — on her level — and plays with her," Austin says.

Fathers and daughters: From tween to teen

It's those pesky "hormonal" years that can often have dads shying away from their moody and sometimes standoffish daughter. When there's a tween girl in the house, "[d]ads should focus on cultivating a trusting relationship so that their daughters feel secure talking with them about what's going on in their lives," Austin explains. "When necessary, dads should apologize and ask for forgiveness, as this both shows respect and love to our daughters and heals the hurts that are inevitable in daily life together."

As a girl continues to grow and her teen years become fraught with complicated issues, dads should continue to work on building a trusting relationship, give affection and support her as she learns more about who she is and what kind of person she wants to become, Austin says.

"It's imperative that, no matter what, dads avoid the temptation to pull away or withdraw during this sometimes-challenging stage of growing up."

A father's influence on a daughter's self-image

A dad's involvement in his daughter's life is a crucial ingredient in the development of a young woman's self-esteem. Austin identifies positive elements of "common sense" parenting for dads so they can help support their daughter's self-image and curb any possibility of low self-esteem: Verbal encouragement, being consistently present in her life, being alert and sensitive to her feelings, taking time to listen to her thoughts and taking an active interest in her hobbies.

"It's important to actually *do* these things, which can sometimes be quite challenging," Austin adds. Direct involvement and encouragement by her father will help diminish a girl's insecurity and increase her confidence in her own abilities.

How dads influence their daughter's relationships

The type of men that women date and have long-term relationships with are also directly related to the kind of relationship a girl has with her father. Obviously, the hope is that the father figure in a girl's life will aim to skew that young lady's opinions of men in a positive way.

"He must, first and foremost, treat his daughter with respect and love. Whether or not he is married to or still together with his daughter's mom, showing respect to her mother is essential as well," explains Austin. "He must also value women as human beings, and not as persons to be used. Daughters will see what their dads believe about women by how they value and respect women, or by how they fail to do so."[9]

I would like to share more of my family background. We have had a generational curse for a long time when it comes to addiction. It has ruined many lives and caused pain to innocent people in their path. With all the addiction in our family, some has ultimately led to imprisonment, homelessness, drug overdose, loss of children, and death from suicide, cancer, and heart attacks. I have experienced a lot of this throughout my life. I felt God reach out to me to do something about this curse. I had to go through a lot of these bad experiences along the way for God to use me. I wanted to beat the odds of this family curse that the devil has taken captive in our family. It has weighed so heavily in my soul to help with setting our family free from bondage of the devil's hands and shackles he has restrained our family for generations.

ASHAMED

Let's talk about the things I have gone through on my journey thus far. I have explained in some of the chapters prior to this that I was emotionally, sexually, and physically abused. These things that I experienced took a toll on my life and confused me so that I acted out and made poor decisions along the way to finding who I was. I have only seen destructive behavior and this pattern of a vicious cycle. I didn't have good mentors in my family to teach me from right from wrong. This doesn't make it an excuse but through my eyes all I saw were unhealthy decisions and poor behavior throughout my adolescent years.

I acted out especially when my father went to prison. I would sneak out in the middle of the night and take my mother's car out for a joy ride, practicing driving in our neighborhood. I had done this many of times at night in my early teen years, but there were two times I ventured out more. I was getting braver and testing the waters when I got caught by police officers. They arrested me and took me to jail. Once I was by myself driving around in the middle of the night looking completely suspicious to a cop, weaving out of my lane. The police officer pulled me over only to find out that I was underage driver when he asked for my license. I remember my heart went to my stomach when I saw those lights turn on and knew I was going to be in serious trouble. The police officer took me to their station and called my mother to come pick me up and he gave me a warning.

In my bright teenager mind, I thought it would be okay to take my mother's car out again. What in the world was I thinking at that time, (obviously I was not because I didn't let myself get scared enough from the first event). So, I thought it was a genius idea to do it again, but this time I got my sweet friend involved in my scheme and we took the car to a park to practice driving. I drove in the wrong lane in the park and a cop noticed. I got pulled over and there I was, arrested again, but this time they handcuffed me. Probably to scare the daylight out of us.

We were crying so hard in the back of the police car. Wow, what was wrong with my mind at that time to make another foolish decision? This was the last time I ever took my mother's car driving in the middle of the night. When I had to go to court to face my crime, I was ashamed of my actions and didn't want to turn out like my father who spent most of his adult life in and out of jail from his bad decision-making. I finally smartened up some and that was the end of my demise.

During these two events. I was trying to cry out for attention for someone to reach out to me and show me that I was loved and cared for. I started drinking with my friends and thought that was cool at the time, but it led to a devasting event. I had some guy friends I knew in a different town about twenty minutes away from where I lived. I called them to come pick up me and my friends who were staying the night with me. They took us back to where they lived and we went to a party and started drinking more, but this time we added marijuana to the mix.

A guy took me out to his truck, and I passed out in his vehicle from being intoxicated and high. He took advantage of me in that state of mind. I was frightened and shocked at what had happened to me. I just wanted to go home. I got out of the truck to go look for my friends to tell them what had happened. I remember being so mad at them for leaving me alone with this guy, even though I knew it wasn't truly their fault. But at the time I felt like that and felt abandoned.

I found a phone to use and started to call people to come pick us up but I couldn't get a hold of anyone. I begged the boys that picked us up to take us home. They finally agreed but the person that took advantage of me while I was impaired was with us when they took us home. I was numb, so sick from drinking and smoking weed; confused and ashamed for allowing myself to be so drunk and high for someone to have sex with me when I was unconscious.

I remember when they drove us home I had to sit on the guy's lap that took advantage of me because there wasn't any room to sit in the car with everyone in the vehicle. He kept kissing me and I just wanted it to stop and get out of the car, so I just let him do it because I was scared if I would make a scene, they wouldn't take us home. I wanted to be far away from this guy. I felt like he was in control and if I made the wrong move that my friends and I would be in danger. I felt like I had to stoop to his level to keep us safe. When we finally got to my house, we were so drunk/high and sick we passed out on the front lawn of my house.

The disappointment ran over me in the morning and I couldn't believe my parents didn't notice what was going on with me. They had no idea we snuck out of the house to go to this party. I wish I had been caught so this event would have never happened to me, but it did. The next day the boy that picked us up that I knew called me because he heard what happened. The boy that raped me was bragging to his friends that he had sex with me. I was so embarrassed when he told me this. He warned me to be careful that he heard this boy that did this to me had HIV. I was devasted along with being distraught and couldn't stop crying. I immediately went to get tested for HIV.

Praise Jesus and his angels looking after me. Imagine for a moment, how scary that would have been for a teenager to have to experience. Your life flashes right in front of your eyes. The thought of your existence was about to end from one tragic event with a terrible decision causing your life to be altered or over.

> O my soul, bless GOD. From head to toe, I'll bless his holy name! O my soul, bless GOD, don't forget a single blessing! He forgives your sins—every one. He heals your diseases—every one. He redeems you from hell—saves your life! He crowns you with love and mercy—a paradise crown. He wraps you in goodness—beauty eternal. He renews your youth—you're always young in his presence.
>
> Psalm 103:2-5, MSG

When You're Between a Rock and a Hard Place

> But now, GOD's Message, the God who made you in the first place, Jacob, the One who got you started,

Israel: "Don't be afraid, I've redeemed you. I've called your name. You're mine. When you're in over your head, I'll be there with you. When you're in rough waters, you will not go down. When you're between a rock and a hard place, it won't be a dead end—Because I am GOD, your personal God, The Holy of Israel, your Savior. I paid a huge price for you: all of Egypt, with rich Cush and Seba thrown in! That's how much you mean to me! *That's* how much I love you! I'd sell off the whole world to get you back, trade the creation just for you.

Isaiah 43:1-4, MSG

After that event happened to me, I steadily got worse. I was trying to numb all the pain from the trauma I had experienced. I felt so lost. I was depressed. I had so much bitterness in my heart asking myself, "Why did all of this happen to me? What did I do that was so horrible for so many things to happen in my life; to be treated so wrong? Why, me?"

My oldest sister was in the wrong crowd. She is seven years older than me. She got into partying heavily. She was drinking and doing a lot of drugs. She introduced me to that world. I let that world take over for several years of my life. I was trying to find meaning in my life. I got out of control. I dated the wrong person for most of my preteen and teenage years. He was verbally abusive, cheated on me all the time, and had an addiction to drugs and alcohol that consumed his life. He was a musician and played the guitar. He was consumed by attention from others. He allowed that world to bring him to a very dark place in his life. He treated me poorly and took advantage of our relationship. He depended on me as well as I depended on him. It became a very unhealthy relationship. It's not one I would recommend anyone to be in. I allowed myself to feel like I was worthless, to where I didn't feel like I deserved anything good, or any happiness. I thought it was the best I was going to get, if I wanted to feel any ounce of love. I thought I should stay in the relationship even if it meant a vicious cycle of abuse. I wasn't getting anything better at home with my family. This was the only attention I was getting in my life and I craved being wanted and loved so I stayed in the relationship for almost ten years off and on, until I found Jesus on November 8, 1995.

It was a long road of healing. I stayed in the relationship three more years after I got saved. It took countless prayer, meditation, crying, being around godly Christian friends for support, and being in church surrounded by other people in love with Jesus for me to see what real healthy living looks like. I read my Bible and self-help books to break the chains of the enemy that had me shackled down for most of my life. I finally had enough courage to leave that relationship and be set free from the bondage of dependency.

To give you a background and a definition what dependency is, this suits me what I was experiencing throughout my childhood. If you don't understand why you are experiencing this type of behavior. This truly explains what a person is experiencing.

DEPENDENT PERSONALITY DISORDER (DPD) is a personality disorder that is characterized by a pervasive psychological dependence on other people. This personality disorder is a long-term condition in which people depend on others to meet their emotional and physical needs, with only a minority achieving normal levels of independence. Dependent personality disorder is a Cluster C personality disorder, characterized by excessive fear and anxiety. It begins by early adulthood, and it is present in a variety of contexts and is associated with inadequate functioning. Symptoms can include anything from extreme passivity, devastation or helplessness when relationships end, avoidance of responsibilities and severe submission.

SIGNS AND SYMPTOMS

People who have dependent personality disorder are overdependent on other people when it comes to making decisions. They cannot make a decision on their own as they need constant approval from other people. Consequently, individuals diagnosed with DPD tend to place needs and opinions of others above their own as they do not have the confidence to trust their decisions. This kind of behavior can explain why people with DPD tend to show passive and clingy behavior. These individuals display a fear of separation and cannot stand being alone. When alone they feel feelings of isolation and loneliness due to their over-whelming dependence on other people. Generally, people with DPD are also pessimistic: they expect the worst out of situations or believe that the worst will happen. They tend to be more introverted and are more sensitive to criticism and fear rejection.[10]

After I graduated from high school and entered the real world, I still made many mistakes. This was a constant battle for me. I couldn't ever stay single. I had back-to-back boyfriends trying to find the right person to fill the void of emptiness, but I kept attracting the wrong men in my life. I was searching to feel validated in relationships. I didn't realize at the time the only true fulfillment to be made whole was surrendering my life completely to Jesus, so He could fill all the broken holes in my heart. I needed His resurrection of healing of all my battle scars and wounds.

There were a lot of things I had to learn, and mostly I had to experience the wrong paths along my walk, searching with Jesus. He had to mend me back together. I am so ashamed of all the decisions I made in my past. Jesus had to pull all the layers back one by one to allow healing for each suffering I had to experience throughout my life.

I had a lot of heartbreaks and sorrow along the way. I want-ed the approval of others; to show I was worth being loved or belonged.

Through those bad relationships I made a very poor deci-sion one night. I was so upset with the person I was dating, and we were drinking. I decided it was a good idea to take the truck while I was drunk. I hopped on the highway where I left him at the gas station because he wanted to drink more with his friends we had been with at the bar and stay out all night. I started to drive reckless then I was thinking to myself, what I am doing? I decided to turn back around on the next exit to go back to the gas station. When I got off at the exit, I over-corrected my wheel and hit the bridge. The truck smashed into the wall on top of the overpass. I was so lucky because if the truck would have gone off the bridge I would be dead today. God saved me. God had something better planned for me.

However, by my wrong choice, I got arrested. But before I got arrested there were people in another vehicle who stopped to check on me. They put me in their car to take me back to the gas station then the police officer pulled up behind them. He pulled me out of the car. He gave me a Standard Field Sobriety Test (SFST) and I failed it. I was arrested for Driving Under the Influence (DUI) of alcohol. The police officer felt so bad for me. I was crying and he put me in his front seat. I was telling him that I deserved this punishment because I knew better what I was doing. I was a Christian and I was making poor decisions. I was talking to him about God. I told him about the horrible relationship I was in. The police officer was giving me encouraging words and told me it was time to leave my boyfriend. The police officer even called the Fire Station to make a complaint against my boyfriend of his actions and what he was doing to me.

I was tired of drinking and tired of the lifestyle we were in. Keep in mind I still loved Jesus and was a Christian but lived a double life on the weekends. I hated my life and the relationship I was in. He was exactly like the other guy I dated for ten years. He was a fireman the spitting image of the other guy. I ask myself many times, "Why in the world did I allow myself to be in another relationship with a person who was verbally abusive, a cheater, and a partier who was just as needy to for the approval of others?" I realized I was dating someone exactly how my father was.

> He who troubles (mismanages) his own house will inherit the wind (nothing), And the foolish will be a servant to the wise-hearted.
>
> Proverbs 11:29, AMP

BEING AWARE OF THE EFFECTS OF A DYSFUNCTIONAL RELATIONSHIP

If you are in an unhealthy relationship now, you may be asking yourself how to get out of the relationship before someone gets hurt. What signs do you need to look for? How do you know when enough is enough, that you need to move on from the relationship? Do you have a parent who may have neglected, or even abused you as a child? Are you feeling unworthy, tainted, dirty, damaged, poisoned, defiled, contaminated, destroyed, ruined, tarnished, or soiled?

I am sure most of us have experienced these types of feelings in our lives. Some more than others.

There are serious long-term effects of dysfunctional relationships. It can gradually get worse which can cause a steady incline of out of control behavior. You may feel that your self-worth is gone, so you stop caring about yourself or people who you hurt in the process. You may even start taking people for granted by taking your anger and rage out on them. You may wake up one morning to find that the only identity you have is that which you have gained from your abuser. The erosion of your self-worth has taken control of your life. You see yourself broken with nowhere to turn to get out of the mess you are in. It can take years of therapy to undo the damage that has been done to you. The seriousness of this can cause personality disorders such as: bipolar disorder, narcissism, psychopath, dissociative identity disorders also known as split personality, neurodevelopment disorder, or antisocial behavior.

We will talk more about behavior disorders in the next chapter. Here is a beautiful song from one of my dear friends from Elementary School that she wrote that reminds me that God is faithful and washes our pain away. It reminds me what I went through was worth it. God will use my story to help others.

You are Faithful
Words and Music: Tara Perry aka Tara Psalmer Music
Lord, I dare offer You empty promises.
But I want to offer all my hopes and dreams
Because my new dream is You.

I used to think this life was mine to have and hold.

Now I know it's better left in Your control

God, my new dream is You

You are faithful...Holy; I want to be

You are Loving...Patient, oh God wash over me.

Cuz You are, The Everlast King

And You are all I'll ever Need. (God)

And so, I humbly bow my knees and pray.

Jesus You are my Everything. (You are my everything)

5

PTSD and Triggers

Because of the surpassing greatness and extraordinary nature of the revelations [which I received from God], for this reason, to keep me from thinking of myself as important, a thorn in the flesh was given to me, a messenger of Satan, to torment and harass me—to keep me from exalting myself! Concerning this I pleaded with the Lord three times that it might leave me; but He has said to me, "My grace is sufficient for you [My lovingkindness and My mercy are more than enough—always available—regardless of the situation]; for [My] power is being perfected [and is completed and shows itself most effectively] in [your] weakness." Therefore, I will all the more gladly boast in my weaknesses, so that the power of Christ [may completely enfold me and] may dwell in me. So I am well pleased with weaknesses, with insults, with distresses, with persecutions, and with difficulties, for the sake of Christ; for when I am weak [in human strength], then I am strong [truly able, truly powerful, truly drawing from God's strength].

2 Corinthians 12:7-10, AMP

Posttraumatic Stress Disorder develops in some people following a traumatic event. The event, or "stressor," could be exposure to death or threatened death, actual or threatened serious injury, or actual or threatened sexual violence. The sufferer may be directly exposed, indirectly exposed through a family member or close friend experiencing the event, or extremely or repeatedly indirectly exposed through his or her work (such as first responders, police officers, military personnel, or social workers). Common trauma experiences are combat, car accidents, natural disasters, abuse, rape, and mass violence. After such an event, most people will show signs of stress such as feeling on edge, anxiety, fear, anger, feelings of depression, a sense of detachment, desire to avoid trauma-related reminders, flashbacks, difficulty sleeping, headaches, changes in appetite, irritability, self-blame, "survivor's guilt," or a sense of numbness. For most people, these reactions lessen and eventually subside with time.

Those who develop PTSD have persistent symptoms for more than one month. Other symptoms for PTSD sufferers include intrusive re-experience of the trauma such as through recurrent, involuntary memories, nightmares, or dissociation; avoidance of trauma-related thoughts or feelings or external reminders; negative changes in thoughts or behavior, including an inability to recall details related to the trauma, persistent negative beliefs about oneself or the world, loss of interest, feelings of alienation, or inability to express positive emotions; and changes in arousal or reactivity such as irritability, aggression, hypervigilance, reckless behavior, or sleep disturbances.[11]

This is a great article I found when I was researching PTSD. If you would like to read more, visit this website in the citation. Reading this identified a lot of what I experienced in my adolescent, teen, and early adult years. I was experiencing a lot of triggers that would pop out of nowhere. Some things would really stress me out. I could feel my agitation to start to rise. I would clam up and it would start to bother me a lot.

I know in the past, when I was in awful relationships and they would start to raise their voice at me, or show signs of anger it would start making me nervous or furious and remind me of when I was living at home with my family. I would shut down or walk away. Many times, I would join in by letting my anger build up and start to lash out as well. Sometimes it would get so bad it was like I was stepping out of my body like (out of body experience) with rage taking over me. My fight mode would come on and my defensive mechanism was to protect myself from harm. I would lose control for a moment, mostly screaming or throwing things in fear. My whole body would be filled by rush of heat. I would start breathing heavily where I couldn't breathe. I would break out in a sweat or I would become dizzy. My body would have an overwhelming surge of stress that came upon me.

At that time, I didn't know what was happening to me. My chest would start to hurt. I thought I was having a heart attack, but I was really having a panic attack caused by so much anxiety. It was such a scary feeling. I thought I needed to be rushed to the hospital. I had to take several deep breaths to calm myself down, but it eventually passed.

Triggers can include sights, sounds, smells, or thoughts that remind you of the traumatic event in some way.

I experienced other triggers when my past relationships cheated on me. I had an overwhelming feeling of being rejected, abandoned, unwanted, not good enough, unloved, and unworthy. I would question myself, "Why was I not good enough? Was I not pretty enough? What did I do to push him to want to cheat on me?" I was battling a lot of self-blame instead of recognizing the real problem wasn't just me, but it was the other person involved in the relationship. I would cling tight as long as I could, so I wouldn't feel alone.

All I wanted in life was to feel loved and wanted, even if it meant sacrificing my beliefs just to feel like I belonged. It tormented me for many years. I felt utter loneliness and self-pity. It kept taking me back to a place when I was younger with my family. That constant insecurity of feeling neglected. As a child my stomach would hurt all the time. I always felt uneasy. I didn't know what was going to happen.

I would struggle developmentally when I was young because of the lack of teaching and parenting at home. Some of the ways I struggled in elementary school was with reading, writing, and math. They had to put me in an extra class for special education to help bring me up to speed in school standards with my age group. I had no one there to help me with the basic English skills needed as a child at home. I had to study more than others. A lot of these basic learning skills were harder for me than for others who were taught by their parents. I had a lot of determination. I wanted to learn. I craved being smart. I didn't want to be like my parents who didn't finish high school. They had a lack of education themselves. I am sure that had to do with some of schoolwork not being taught to me.

Below are some warning signs to watch for children that are being neglected. After reading these it makes sense what my body was experiencing. I read this on a website published with American Academy of Pediatrics.

- Fearful behavior (nightmares, unusual fears, depression)
- Abdominal pain, bed-wetting (especially if the child has already been toilet trained)
- Attempts to run away
- Extreme sexual behavior that seems inappropriate for the child's age
- Sudden change in self-confidence
- Headaches or stomachaches with no medical cause
- Abnormal fears, increased nightmares
- School failure

- Extremely passive or aggressive behavior
- Desperately affectionate behavior or social withdrawal
- Big appetite and stealing food

PHYSICAL SIGNS
- Any injury (bruise, burn, fracture, abdominal or head injury) that cannot be explained
- Failure to gain weight (especially in infants) or sudden dramatic weight gain
- Genital pain or bleeding
- A sexually transmitted disease[12]

Throughout my life there were so many ups and downs that I experienced. It caused self-esteem issues along with a bad self-image. I wanted to prove I was worth something. When having childhood trauma, it can damage the way you view yourself. I never felt content in anything. My self-confidence was very low. I had difficulty in relationships. I would either cling too closely or I would avoid becoming too attached so I would sabotage my relationship before I got hurt by the other person in my life.

When we are children, we are programmed at a very young age. Children are like sponges that take everything in that good or bad. We learn from our parents, caregivers, and peers around us. Living in the abusive environment I had at home, I developed a caregiver personality. I wanted to protect others from harm, especially my siblings and cousins. I didn't know the meaning of how one should be treated with love, respect, security, value and kindness.

As I got older. I over-compensated for my lack of feeling wanted by being desperate in need to achieve in my academics, succeed to be the best at my job, to gain recognition and always needed to feel validated by rewards of my success. This would help me to keep myself from thinking about the real root of my problems. I would give 100% in everything; I was highly competitive and driven to be a more successful person than others around me. I was driven to make money, to have nice cars, home, clothes, and a perfect image. I struggled with not being good enough, so this caused me to be out of control in these areas to prove my worthiness to belong.

IMPRESSION MANAGEMENT BEHAVIOR

I realized I had somewhat of a problem to prove my self-worth. In order to prove that I was the best, I would put on a façade. I didn't want people to see the brokenness I felt inside so in public I would put on a fake smile, so people didn't know the overwhelming pain I felt. I would misrepresent myself to show a different impression of who I was. I would boast about my accomplishments to make myself feel better, or for people to not ask questions about me but for them to notice more of my accomplishments. I would put on a mask. I lacked confidence in myself. I was always scared about becoming a failure. My parents failed me, and I didn't want to fail myself by becoming my parents. I would lose touch with reality when work would consume me. I made terrible decisions.

I would dress up to attract men. I would wear more inappropriate clothing for them to notice me. When I did this, I would attract the wrong men and it was dangerous and reckless behavior. This would help me when I was in business. I would use my looks to gain more attention which helped me in my job in marketing/sales to gain more business and more clients.

SELF-PRESENTATION BEHAVIOR

DEFINITION

"Self-presentation refers to how people attempt to present themselves to control or shape how others (called the audience) view them. It involves expressing oneself and behaving in ways that create a desired impression. Self-presentation is part of a broader set of behaviors called *impression management*. Impression management refers to the controlled presentation of information about all sorts of things, including information about other people or events. Self-presentation refers specifically to information about the self."[13]

When I was younger, we were very poor. We didn't have a nice home and it was cluttered all the time. I was extremely embarrassed of my home. My mother made sure I had nice clothes so people wouldn't know we didn't have much money. She would use her credit cards to get me nice things. When my mother would take me to school before I got my license, I would sneak down real low in the passenger seat so no one could see me. I waited to get out of the car until I knew no one was around that

I knew. Kids were mean and I didn't want to get made fun of for being poor. My mother's car was in bad shape. Paint was missing and basically it was a clunker.

In school, nobody knew I was poor other than my closet friends that were in elementary with me. I remember one time a friend offered to take me home after I had a sleepover with them. They were wealthy and I was afraid if they saw where I lived that they wouldn't be friends with me any longer. I was afraid they would judge me. They would always compliment me at school about my clothes and how cute I looked. So you can see why I was reluctant and didn't want them to see where I lived.

When we got into my neighborhood down the street I asked them to drop me off and I would walk the rest of the way. They told me that wasn't necessary, but I begged them to please do it. I didn't want them to see where I lived. I was ashamed of my home. They agreed and dropped me off. I made sure they were long gone before I walked up to my house, so they didn't see where I was living.

When I was sixteen, I got a job working as a waitress. I worked so hard to save up money. I got my license and got a nice car so when I would go to my high school people would think I was wealthy. I presented myself differently in school when I would walk in through the front doors of mid-high. I was ashamed of my upbringing. I didn't want people to meet my parents, especially my father being an alcoholic and a mean drunk. You can see how I wanted to keep my self-presentation of quiet. I showed them only what they wanted to see on the outside, but wouldn't let people close enough to see the inside.

These are more signs of triggers to watch for you, a loved one, or a friend who has been abused. This is another great article to pull more information up on this from WebMd.

THOUGHTS AND EMOTIONS: The way you felt during a traumatic event (afraid, helpless, or stressed) could cause symptoms.

THINGS: Seeing an object that reminds you of the trauma can cue your PTS Symptoms.

SCENTS: Smells are strongly tied to memories. For instance, someone who survived a fire might become upset from the smoky smell of a barbecue. Another way if you were raped or molested and a certain smell pops up somewhere that reminds you of your perpetrator.

PLACES: Returning to the scene of a trauma is often a trigger. Or a type of place, like a dark hallway, may be enough to bring on a reaction.

TV SHOWS, NEWS REPORTS, AND MOVIES: Seeing a similar trauma often sets off symptoms. This includes scenes from a television show or movie, or a news report.

FEELINGS: Some sensations, such as pain, are triggers. For survivors of assault, a touch on a certain body part may lead to a flashback.

SOUNDS: Hearing specific noises, songs, or voices may bring back memories of the trauma. For example, hearing a car backfire may remind a veteran of gunfire.

TASTES: The taste of something, like alcohol, may remind you of a traumatic event.

SITUATIONS: You may tie scenarios with the trauma. For instance, being stuck in an elevator might remind you of feeling trapped after a car accident.

ANNIVERSARIES: It's often hard to go through a date marked by trauma without remembering it, as is the case for many survivors of the terrorist attacks on September 11, 2001.

WORDS: Reading or hearing certain words could cue your PTSD.[14]

FEAR OF ABANDONMENT

I wanted to explain a little bit more what I struggled with. I hated being left alone all the time when I was younger. I had to step into a role to be the parent to my siblings and my cousins.

My parents were gone all the time. I was the oldest child in the house. I had a bitter heart toward my parents. I was frustrated that they were so caught up in themselves and their problems that I felt like we were a burden to them. I would try to avoid those feelings in my home by taking off from my house and staying with friends all the time. I hated the feelings of constant torment of fear and anxiety. I would look for ways to make my feelings go away.

I had a problem with dating boys one after another. I had a problem trusting them. I would sometimes cheat on them in order to not feel rejected. I would go to extreme measures to avoid any unwanted feelings of pain so I would get into a pattern seeking unhealthy relationships. Especially with guys who had issues within themselves or in their homes. If they didn't know who Jesus was, I wanted to come in and try to save them. I liked the challenge of helping someone who was lost. Maybe because that was how I felt.

I wanted someone desperately to reach out to me to guide me. I took on the role to do this for others. I would get attached way too quickly in my relationships, then when I saw warning signs about a year into the relationship, I would try to move out just as quickly to avoid being left or abandoned first. I had a hard time committing to relationships very long. At first, I would work so hard to please that person in the beginning, they would do the same to me. Then I would notice signs that reminded me of my father and it would bring unwanted triggers in my core. I couldn't take the pain. I would start to blame myself when things didn't work out in the relationship. I would try to stay in the relationship, but when it was getting too unhealthy or causing extreme anxiety, I would sabotage the relationship by cheating on them with another person just to make an excuse to get out of the relationship. This was a vicious cycle I was in for a long time.

SELF-PRESERVATION

I tried to hold onto my self-preservation as long as I could. I went into survival mode in my life. I kicked it into full gear trying to keep the fear and the guilt from coming out where it was entangled in my soul, and eventually it was starting to seep through into my real world where others around me started to see. Eventually the lie became too much that I let my hurts come to the surface. I withdrew from others and became a hermit, depressed from all the bad decisions I was making. The pain became too much to bear on my own. The burden was too much to carry. I didn't want to harbor anymore resentment of my past avengers, excusers, and abusers. I wanted to be set free from the agony. I needed help.

The constant back forth trying to live a good life, then allowing the shame to take a hold of me of all the damaging things that had happened to me, along with what I did to myself by what I allowed to enter in my life-which was sin that took over me. I wanted to protect my image and my self-worth but most of all my relationship with Jesus Christ. I wanted my soul to be healed once and for all.

I went to church October 3, 2004 on a Wednesday night. That night I truly gave my heart to the Lord. That time it wasn't just a word, it was something that was truly inside of me that I really wanted to do in my life. I was full of disgust at the things I was doing to myself and I had no one to blame but myself. At that time, I felt I was living in somebody else's body. I came to the realization that the deep wounded hurts that I had not been able to overcome or forget trapped me.

I struggled through this all my life. I used things to make me feel better for the time being, but by doing those things it put me bigger pit. It was like a hurricane that swooped me up. I was trying to climb up out of the pit of despair and put the pieces together on my own. But it wasn't working without God's hand. I had to take courage by stepping out in faith and positioning myself in another direction. I had allowed the devil to take a hold of me for a long time. If I avoided that wrong turn I may have steered in the right path. However, I took a detour instead and allowed my hurts to surface. I struggled with good vs. evil in my soul. I allowed the battle in my mind to become so strong that it almost destroyed me. Jesus opened my eyes to see there was a whole new level of love and meaning in my life and that is with Him. He is my healer, restorer, confidant, and savior.

So, as God's own chosen people, who are holy [set apart, sanctified for His purpose] and well-beloved [by God Himself], put on a heart of compassion, kindness, humility, gentleness, and patience [which has the power to endure whatever injustice or unpleasantness comes, with good temper]; bearing graciously with one another, and willingly forgiving each other if one has a cause for complaint against another; just as the Lord has forgiven you, so should you forgive. Beyond all these things put on and wrap yourselves in [unselfish] love, which is the perfect bond of unity [for everything is bound together in agreement when each one seeks the best for others]. Let the peace of Christ [the inner calm of one who walks daily with Him] be the controlling factor in your hearts [deciding and settling questions that arise]. To this peace indeed you were called as members in one body [of believers]. And be thankful [to God always]. Let the [spoken] word of Christ have its home within you [dwelling in your heart and mind— permeating every aspect of your being] as you teach [spiritual things] and admonish and train one another with all wisdom, singing psalms and hymns and spiritual songs with thankfulness in your hearts to God. Whatever you do [no matter what it is] in word or deed, do everything in the name of the Lord Jesus [and in dependence on Him], giving thanks to God the Father through Him.

Colossians 3:12-17, AMP

Prayer:

Lord, we have been blinded by so many things. We were lost but now we are found. We desire to know you more Lord, to cleanse our souls and make us new again. I pray for the righteousness of all Your people as we rejoice in Your Holy Spirit. Take away all the evil and pain that we once felt. We bow down and rejoice in Your name that You will take our broken heart and soul by restoring us brand new again. Teach Your people of Your ways by guiding them the way You want them to live. Help us to start a new life feeling free from the enemy. Help us to only rely on You and no one else to fulfill our needs. Remind us to not rely on mankind for satisfaction to feel loved or wanted, but to rely only on You to make us feel complete. Lord it is only You that fills our broken hearts with joy. I pray for women out there who feel the only way they will be happy is to have a man in their life. I pray that You will fill the hole in their hearts and allow them to only date You Lord, so You can teach them what a healthy relationship is all about. Bring clarity to what true love is so one day You will prepare the woman's soul the right way to be treated like a princess. We know You will always take care of us. Help us to listen and obey Your commands. Remind us of Your pure love that we will always honor You til death do us part forever and ever. We count on You, Jesus, and trust You to help us to be restored in all areas of our lives. I know You will bless us for our faithfulness and patience. Remind us to not be too impatient that we need something or someone right now. Your name we pray, Amen.

Friends, don't allow yourselves to get exhausted and fall apart by the pressure you put on yourself. Trust in yourself and wait patiently for God's direction over your life. God is working on your soul as we speak. He may be telling you to stay still so he can work his miracles in you. Whatever burden you are having right now, remind yourself that you are loved and mature enough to receive God's spiritual blessings He has in store for you. Put your worries in a box and lock them up. Throw away the key and never look back. The Lord will answer your prayers when the time is right. Never be blinded again by this world. Quit worrying about what everybody thinks of you. The only one you should worry about is our precious Savior. He sees your beauty by His replication of His own image. We are His greatest accomplishment.

> Let us rejoice and shout for joy! Let us give Him glory *and* honor, for the marriage of the Lamb has come [at last] and His bride (the redeemed) has prepared herself.
>
> Revelation 19:7, AMP

I had to learn the hard way by crashing and burning on the runway. Now God has given me the ability to land smoothly. He gave me the tools to forgive myself and move on. I learned to put all my trust in God. God will get us through anything if we give our whole heart to Him. He has healed all malicious thoughts, actions, and pain I encountered.

If you are struggling in a marriage from the weight of pain you carried over in the relationship from the past hurts, abuse, neglect, rejection, trauma, burdens of being unwanted, un-loved, or any disorders that you are struggling with–it's okay to get professional help, to seek counseling to work out any struggles you are having. I have done this for many years, and this has helped me tremendously with my healing process.

Learn in your marriage to love one another. Respect your spouse the same way Christ respects and cares for you. When something is bothering you, learn to trust and communicate. It is very important in the relationship. Speak kindly as the way you would want to be treated. Remember: don't let your mouth get a foothold of you with anger or triggers that arise in you. Never go to bed still angry with each other. Always rejoice and speak life in the marriage. Speak positive words of affirmation. Cast out all fear or pain that comes from the darkness and tries to bring a barrier or a wall in your marriage. Get rid of your corrupted thoughts and restore them with the love of Jesus and the Holy Spirit that feeds your soul with new life. Jesus has reformed you with the light of your heavenly Father.

> If in fact you have [really] heard Him and have been taught by Him, just as truth is in Jesus [revealed in His life and personified in Him], that, regarding your previous way of life, you put off your old self [completely discard your former nature], which is being corrupted through deceitful desires, and be continually renewed in the spirit of your mind [having a fresh, untarnished mental and spiritual attitude], and put on the new self [the regenerated and renewed nature], created in God's image, [godlike] in the righteousness and holiness of the truth [living in a way that expresses to God your gratitude for your salvation].

Therefore, rejecting all falsehood [whether lying, defrauding, telling half-truths, spreading rumors, any such as these], speak truth each one with his neighbor, for we are all parts of one another [and we are all parts of the body of Christ]. Be angry [at sin—at immorality, at injustice, at ungodly behavior], yet do not sin; do not let your anger [cause you shame, nor allow it to] last until the sun goes down. And do not give the devil an opportunity [to lead you into sin by holding a grudge, or nurturing anger, or harboring resentment, or cultivating bitterness]. The thief [who has become a believer] must no longer steal, but instead he must work hard [making an honest living], producing that which is good with his own hands, so that he will have something to share with those in need. Do not let unwholesome [foul, profane, worthless, vulgar] words ever come out of your mouth, but only such speech as is good for building up others, according to the need and the occasion, so that it will be a blessing to those who hear [you speak]. And do not grieve the Holy Spirit of God [but seek to please Him], by whom you were sealed and marked [branded as God's own] for the day of redemption [the final deliverance from the consequences of sin]. Let all bitterness and wrath and anger and clamor [perpetual animosity, resentment, strife, fault-finding] and slander be put away from you, along with every kind of malice [all spitefulness, verbal abuse, malevolence]. Be kind and helpful to one another, tender-hearted [compassion-ate, understanding], forgiving one another [readily and freely], just as God in Christ also forgave you.

Ephesians 4:21-32, AMP

6

Guilt, Shame, and Regret

If we [freely] admit that we have sinned *and* confess our sins, He is faithful and just [true to His own nature and promises], and will forgive our sins and cleanse us *continually* from all unrighteousness [our wrongdoing, everything not in conformity with His will and purpose].

1 John 1:9, AMP

He shall again have compassion on us; He will subdue *and* tread underfoot our wickedness [destroying sin's power]. Yes, you will cast all our sins into the depths of the sea.

Micah 7:19, AMP

This is one that I struggled with throughout my life. All the bad decisions I made have haunted me for many years of my life. I needed to release my guilt by giving my regrets and shame to God. There are times I had a flashback of something

I did, then my heart sank to my stomach and I immediately felt ill. This happens to most people when they make a wrong decision in their life. We will go through consequences of our behavior first to learn and understand that what we have done is not God's will for our life. We may have to experience pain and suffering for God to change our hearts. He needs to heal our pain that ruptured our heart and caused mini holes. God must fill in those holes with the blood of Christ to restore our flesh new to be one with Him.

> Just as Christ loved the church and gave himself up
> for her to make her holy, cleansing her by the washing with water through the word.
>
> Ephesians 5:25-26, NIV

We as the Church, the Body of Christ, must allow ourselves to be forgiven so God can work in us His masterpiece of our lives. He has restored the real us God has called us to be. Please read this Article that was written by Jon Bloom, *Staff Writer*, at DesiringGod.org.

These stories capture the real pain caused by shame from mistakes made by God's people. We all make mistakes. We must have the ability to admit and confess with our mouths to acknowledge the wrongdoing and ask for forgiveness. God forgives all who ask and repent of their ways.

BREAKING THE POWER OF SHAME

"Her life was a wreck. After five failed marriages she stopped with the formalities. She came to the well when the sun blazed so she could draw water alone and hide from the comments, the whispers, and the condemning looks (John 4).

He was a powerful man who abused his power to sleep with another man's wife. But he got her pregnant. And out of fear of exposing his wickedness he tried to hide behind a cover-up that turned murderous (2 Samuel 11).

She had suffered from a vaginal hemorrhage for twelve years. All that time: unclean, uncomfortable, and uncomforted. She saw Jesus heal others and longed to receive his touch. But how could she ask him in front of the whole crowd? So, she sought to hide in anonymity by just touching the fringe of his robe (Luke 8:43-48).

These are three biblical portraits of people who tried to hide their shame in the wrong places. But the wonderful thing is that all three experienced God's power to break shame's hold over them and set them free. And this wonderful experience can also be ours.

WHAT GIVES SHAME POWER

Shame has plagued us since Adam and Eve bit into the fruit and realized they were naked. Their first instinct was to hide from each other and God (Genesis

3:7-11). And no wonder. They now stood guilty before God and were vulnerable to each other and Satan in a whole new horrible way. Suddenly, they were sinful, weak, damaged people living in a dangerous world. They found themselves under God's righteous judgment (Genesis 3:17-19; John 3:19; Romans 6:23), exposed to other sinners' sinful judgment and rejection, and wide-open to the condemning accusations of the evil one (Revelation 12:10).

We also live in this dangerous world and have the same instinct to hide ourselves.

Because sin is alive in our bodies (Romans 7:23) and because we are beset with weakness (Hebrews 5:2), the kind of shame we often experience is a potent combination of failure and pride. We fail morally (sin), we fail due to our limitations (weakness), and we fail because the creation is subject to futility and doesn't work right (Romans 8:20). We also fail to live up to other people's expectations. And because we are full of sinful pride, we are ashamed of our failures and weaknesses, and will go to almost any length to hide them from others.

This means pride-fueled shame can wield great power over us. It controls significant parts of our lives and consumes precious energy and time in avoiding exposure.

HIDING IN THE WRONG PLACE

Like the woman at the well, King David, and the hemorrhaging woman, our shame frequently encourages us to hide in the wrong places.

We hide in our homes or away from our homes. We hide in our rooms and in our offices. We hide in housework, yard work, and garage puttering. We hide behind computers and phones and newspapers and magazines. We hide behind earphones and Netflix and ESPN. We hide behind fashion facades, education facades, career facades, Facebook facades, and pulpit facades. We hide in busyness and procrastination. We hide in outright lies or diversionary conversation. We hide behind sullenness and humor. We hide behind bravado and timidity. We hide in extroversion and introversion.

You see, we have our own noontime well visits, our sin cover-ups, and our anonymous touches. Pride moves us to use whatever we can to hide our shame.

THE KEY TO BREAKING SHAME'S POWER

But just because pride moves us to hide our shame in the wrong places doesn't mean that our instinct to hide is completely wrong. It isn't. We do need a place to hide, but we need to hide in the right place.

And there is only one place to hide that offers the protection we seek, where all our shame is covered, and we no longer need to fear: the refuge of Jesus

Christ Hebrews 6:18-20). Jesus's death and resurrection are the only remedy for the shame we feel over our grievous sin-failures (Hebrews 9:26). There is nowhere else to go with our sin; there is no other atonement (Acts 4:12). But if we hide in Jesus, he provides us a complete cleansing (1 John 1:9). And when that happens, all God's promises, which find their yes in Christ (2 Corinthians 1:20), become ours if we believe and receive them. And the grace that flows from these promises to us through faith are all-sufficient and abounding and provide for all our other shameful weaknesses and failures (2 Corinthians 9:8).

The key to breaking the power of pride-fueled shame is the superior power of humility-fueled faith in the work of Christ and the promises of Christ. Shame pronounces us guilty and deficient. Jesus pronounces us guiltless and promises that his grace will be sufficient for us in all our weaknesses (2 Corinthians 12:9-10). Christ is all (Colossians 3:11). As we trust Jesus as our righteousness (Philippians 3:9) and our provider of everything we need (Philippians 4:19), Shame will lose its power over us.

That's what happened to the woman at the well. She listened to Jesus and believed in him, and her sin-wrecked life was redeemed, and her shame destroyed.

That's what happened to King David. He confessed his sin and repented (2 Sam 12:13) and trusted the pre-incarnate Christ, and his guilt and shame, which was great, was imputed to Christ and paid for in full.

And that's what happened to the hemorrhaging woman. Jesus did make her tell the crowd about her shame, and in doing so she received the healing and cleansing she needed. Jesus made her shame a show-case of his grace.

And this wonderful experience can also be ours. All it requires is child-like, wholehearted belief in Jesus (John 14:1)"[15]

GUILT

Let's discuss this topic first. This one I struggled with feeling guilty for leaving my siblings and my cousins behind with the abuse in the home when I was sixteen years old. I couldn't take the constant misery, screaming, cussing, negativity, neglect, and lack of love or showing affection.

When I was at that age, I wanted to get out of the home as quickly as possible. I took an opportunity to take off fast and be away from the madness that was exploding in the home.

When I was at that age, I was a new Christian. I started to see what it looked like to have some normalcy in my life by watching others the way they should be treated. I longed for that same connection with my family the way I connected in the church. I didn't understand why my parents couldn't get it together at that time. My youth pastor and his wife lived a couple houses down. I rode to church with them sometimes. His wife was so loving and kind to me. I remember going to their home and making a carrot cake for my pastor to show my appreciation for his guidance and teachings.

They knew the situation I was in along with my siblings and cousins. They were so loving and kind, so good to me along with the little ones in our home. They knew how difficult it was for all of us. They were so good to me. They encouraged me to look at life differently through the love of Jesus' eyes. The love they had for each other was incredible. They showed me by their actions what a strong foundation of a marriage looked like. God gave them a true gift for kids. At the time they didn't have kids yet, so their kids were the youth of our church.

At that time, I was craving God and soaking up as much as I could learn about God. I went to church a lot. They sponsored me to go to church camps when they had them. They knew my parents didn't have the money to spend for me to go, so they sponsored those camps for me to go. Which was an amazing blessing. Those camps really changed my heart by being around other Christians in fellowship serving and loving the Lord.

The more I got involved in church the less time I was spending at home. I started to notice my life was not okay for any child to live in. I would stay at my friend's house a lot. I was creating as much distance as possible from my parents which resulted in creating a barrier with my siblings and cousins. I felt terrible about this. I wanted to be around people who loved Jesus. They were so happy to be around. They were full of life. Every time I would come home it was like they sucked all the laughter out of me when I walked in my front door. The immediate chaos started as soon as my feet hit the carpet of my living room floor.

The angels were working extra hard in overtime for me, battling the demons that were lurking in my home. I was a new Christian that was fragile and could be easily persuaded in the wrong direction. I remember crying myself to sleep sometimes; begging God to stop this torment of pain we all were experiencing. I would lay awake outside on the porch at night, looking at the stars, praying to God and asking for mercy in our home; pleading with God to break the chains of this vicious cycle of dysfunctional behavior. I felt constantly tormented in the home, and helpless that I couldn't help my parents out by taking away the pain they felt.

My father was so depressed from his sister taking her own life that it consumed him. It was a plague of heavy rain cloud storming above his head. The enemy was winning at the time and making my father's life a living hell on earth. My mother was reaping the wounds of my father's torment and consequences of his actions that allowed my mother to feel numbness and defeat. The lion was creeping in slowing and steadily in my parents' lives. They couldn't see up from down because he twisted their bodies and caused dizziness in their eyesight that their equilibrium was off. They didn't know which way they were coming and going.

This frightened me. I could feel the evil presence in the home, and I didn't want anything more to do with it. I remember multiple times laying in my bed and feeling something lurking in the shadows. Fear was rising in my body. I felt an evil presence in the home at times that felt so real to me. I have woken up a lot feeling something over me and opened my eyes to see something floating above me. I couldn't tell at the time what it was, but I knew it wasn't right.

There were other times I woke up and saw the peace of God's angels over me. I would wake up at night and see in my room the sparkling shape of a figure and I knew it was God's angels protecting me. This constant fight was happening all around me at night when I was sleeping. There was spiritual warfare happening in our home. Sometimes I didn't understand how we made it out alive from the wreckage we were living in. I thank God that he kept them there to keep all of us safe from being in harm by my father's raft of temper from his drunken stupor.

There were many times my father would pass out with a cigarette in his hand and burn his t-shirts, sheets, and our couch from the burning fire on the cigarette. God kept us safe from the harm of fire. This right here reminds me of hell. The fire blazed so strong and you could feel the heat on your face from the flames, but God was holding us back from being burnt by the flame and the touch of Satan.

Since I was a little girl, I could always sense presence around me. Not as much now, but I did when I was young and throughout my early twenties. I think God gave me that extra peace of comfort that I needed to get through the pain I was in. I know to others it may sound silly but for me that is what I needed to get through the hell I was living in. Satan was trying to get me off course from God so he worked hard on my weaknesses. This is where I started to feel shame.

SHAME

As I mentioned in one of my earlier chapters, I was in a relationship off and on for ten years. This boy was my weakness to my core. It seemed like as soon as I felt things were going well, Satan would put this individual back in my life to get me off course to the destination that God was directing me toward. I battled for a long time to feel that love. This person gave me the attention that I needed to fill that void in my life when I was most vulnerable. The closer I would get to God; the harder Satan would hit and attack me head on by sending him back in my life.

This relationship was most definitely not healthy. It was a love/hate relationship. I thought I loved him, but hated who he represented by the lifestyle he was living. He pretty much lived a lifestyle like a musician who loved sex, drugs, drinking, and craved the attention of others from people worshipping him when he sang and played his guitar. When he started partying, he would stay up all night long binge drinking, doing drugs, and singing. He couldn't stop when he started. He loved the admiration. This was the definition of my father, other than the drugs and singing.

I had googly eyes for him when he sang and played his guitar. I was smitten by his looks and he was older than me by two years. I thought he was the coolest guy at the time. He got along with my father, which I thought was nice, but when those two would get together they would drink together and stay up all night. They would feed off each other's drinking problems and they would do it for hours. This would make me so furious and disgusted by their behavior, but for some reason I would stay put in the relationship no matter how miserable I was.

There was a church camp that I went to that got me away from the sin and shame I was living. When I would return home from church camp, I broke off our relationship when my strength and courage was back from God. I was heavily convicted at camp for my actions and the place I was in. I rededicated my commitment back to God. I would start doing well when the boy was not in my life. I could see clearly, and nothing was shadowing my vision. I started to get involved more in church, hanging out with my church friends to keep me on the right track.

I would go to small groups within our church and learn the books in the Bible from Old to New Testament. I had no clue mind you on the Bible, nor how to read or understand what the books of the Bible meant. However, I was eager and pleased to learn. I was embarrassed at first when introduced to the Bible in one of the Sunday morning groups. The teacher asked me to read something in the Bible and I didn't know where the book was in the Bible. This was the first time really using it. My sweet teacher encouraged me to read the Bible. She was so kind and patient.

I lacked self-esteem and was not confident in my reading skills in the Bible. This is one thing I needed to learn: self-confidence. I struggled with this a lot. I worried what others would think of me. This skill was never taught to me growing up, so this was a foreign topic for me. She taught me so much from being in her classes. I looked up to her. I loved how much she lived for Jesus in everything she did. I wanted to be like her. She was poised with strength and confidence. She radiated God's image. The tranquility of love of Jesus spilled over her with gracefulness. By watching her it gave me peace to let go of my fear.

I constantly fed my spirit with reading. I read out loud and prayed with my friends at the altar. I started to build confidence in myself and started to pray out loud with them on Wednesday night service for the youth group. I was high on life and happier than I had ever been. I started dating Christian boys in the church who were on fire with Jesus. It was so exciting.

Then I made a terrible decision one day and went to a boy's house while his parents were gone. We hung out and we made a terrible decision together when we were not supervised. We were intimate and he lost his virginity. His parents found out and he had to break it off with me. I felt instant shame and regret for my actions. I was so sick to my stomach. This hit me hard. I was so caught up in my fantasy world by his attention he was giving me, and his sister being my discipleship-team leader in my Bible study group that I looked up to so much, and I was getting close to his family. I took for granted the relationship I had with them.

I was so distraught by my actions. All I wanted to do was to live my life right, but the sin of my past world crept in and tempted me. I allowed sin back into my life and made selfish decisions that had consequences ahead that crossed a line I couldn't get back from. The shame became so powerful that regret started to take over all my thoughts. This distracted me so much. I slipped away from God and started to date my ex-boyfriend again. I was a mess and needed Jesus more than ever. I needed His hand to hold onto mine and bring me back to the promise land.

> Do not be conformed to this world, but be transformed by the renewal of your mind, that by testing you may discern what is the will of God, what is good and acceptable and perfect.
>
> Romans 12:2, ESV

REGRET

The burden of my heart was so heavy it led me to take the wrong turn. I was mumbling and complaining that I was like God's people. Moses was leading God's people out of slavery to the promised land, but God's people complained, grumbled, and questioned Moses' directions. They lacked faith that they spent forty years in the wilderness when the freedom of joy was just around the corner. They were so caught up in the past that they complained about the lack of food they had, being tired, and growing weary waiting for Moses to return from his forty-day fast with God up on the Mountain.

God provided two tablets made of stone for His people to abide by God's law. This was held up on Mt. Sinai and on the two stones the 10 Commandments were written. People started worshipping false gods and built a golden calf. When Moses returned, he was so furious at God's people that he threw the 10 Commandments at the people who made the golden calf. They were blinded by the bitterness that led them down the wrong road through treacherous boulders which caused their journey to be so long that it lasted forty years. If their hearts were right and followed God's commands, their journey could have been only a year long.

When Moses lost his temper, God punished Moses that he could not enter into the promised land, along with his brother Aaron for not controlling God's people while Moses was gone. Moses stripped Aaron of his priestly garments and released him of his duties. Moses was granted a view of the promised land from afar in Mt. Nebo but never was able to step foot in the land with milk and honey. God took Moses and ascended him to Heaven. Joshua, Moses' assistant, completed the task for Moses that led God's people to the land called Canaan.

Can you imagine working so hard for so many years to bring justice for God's people, along with serving God faithfully, and following God's will for freedom for his people, then making a terrible decision that changes everything? I am sure once Moses lost his temper, he had instant regret in his heart. The frustration got the best of him with all the disobedience of God's people and in a moment of weakness he lashed out. When his behavior took a toll on him, he was not able to experience the blessing of God's promised land.

I am sure many of you can relate. How many people in this world make bad decisions and have the immediate regret what they did? I know I have, and I have done this more times that I can count. God has mercy on my soul and for all His people. God knows we are sinners. He has compassion for us. That is why He sent Jesus here on earth in living form to experience what all of us feel living in this world full of sin.

He gave us an opportunity to bring restoration in our hearts by receiving Jesus in our hearts so we can spend all eternity with Him in Heaven. What amazing God! We are so lucky that He loves us with unconditional love. I feel honored and joyful when I think of what He has done for me and for God's people even when our eyes are clouded with sin. He has the purest intent for our wellbeing.

> And Moses said, "When the LORD gives you in the evening meat to eat and in the morning bread to the full, because the LORD has heard your grumbling that you grumble against him—what are we? Your grumbling is not against us but against the LORD.
>
> Exodus 16:8, ESV

> And the people complained in the hearing of the Lord about their misfortunes, and when the Lord heard it, his anger was kindled, and the fire of the Lord burned among them and consumed some outlying parts of the camp. Then the people cried out to Moses, and Moses prayed to the Lord, and the fire died down. So

the name of that place was called Taberah, because
the fire of the Lord burned among them. Now the
rabble that was among them had a strong craving.
And the people of Israel also wept again and said, "Oh
that we had meat to eat!"

Numbers 11:1-4, ESV

SELF-PITY

Back to my self-pity party...I was mad about everything. I
started heavily partying, being reckless and sexually active
with my boyfriend. We moved in with each other when I was
seventeen and he was nineteen. I was mad at the world. I felt
like my Christian friends abandoned me, the church failed me
by not reaching out to me when I was seeking help, and I felt
betrayed. This was a trigger for me, and it felt like the world
and everyone was against me, so I threw my hands in the air
and decided not to care.

I would say, "Why should I care? My parents didn't care for
me...I was sexually molested, and no one loved me enough to
notice...I was crying for help and no one was listening...I was
sneaking out, drinking, smoking weed, and no one turned to
look my way to pull me out of the pit of despair."

I went into a deep hole of depression until I finally started to
quit feeling sorry for myself. I was able to open my eyes again.
Little by little I started to go back to church. I was still living in
full sin by living with my boyfriend at the time. I got so tired of
the partying. I was miserable. I slowly started to distance my-

self from him. I was working a lot to support myself and finish high school. I started to notice he was stealing money from me to support his habits. He was not working.

Basically, I was taking care of everything and supported both of us with my income. He couldn't keep a job because his addiction to drinking and doing drugs was more important to him than holding down a job. I finally got so sick of it. He was cheating on me and I found out. He wasn't coming home at night. I cheated on him and kicked him out and broke off our relationship. This was the end of us. I finally put my foot down even when he tried to come back around. I never went back to him.

So, you can see I was a hot mess. My intentions were good, but my actions were terrible. I needed help. The only way this was going to happen was to get some counseling and get healed inside and out from all the pain and tragic events that occurred in my life. The regret came full-fledged in my life. I was so mad at myself for making so many bad decisions. I talked poorly to myself. I was in pain in my soul from battling all sorts of sin. I couldn't do it alone any longer. I needed Jesus and his forgiveness of all my actions.

I had to remind myself it was not the end of my journey. God is my restoration. He will conqueror my enemy. I took a step of courage to move forward and believe in myself. I could get through any pain that came my way. I started reading the One-Year Bible. One book stood out to me the most at that time and that was the book of Job. This was a powerful awakening to my spirit that I needed so the Holy Spirit could rise in my soul to bring forgiveness and healing.

Also, this was my journey to learn how to love myself. This was not an easy task. This took many years to achieve. It was slow baby steps to take, but the more I took the steps, the easier it started to become more natural to me. The hardest part of my journey was trying to teach my brain the right type of living and to exercise my thought process with constant self-talk by speaking God's love over my life daily. We will get into more of that in a later chapter. Please read this summary that I included below. I found a quick summary of the book of Job that you can read.

SUMMARY OF JOB

"Job is a wealthy man living in a land called Uz with his large family and extensive flocks. He is "blameless" and "upright," always careful to avoid doing evil (1:1). One day, Satan ("the Adversary") appears before God in heaven. God boasts to Satan about Job's goodness, but Satan argues that Job is only good because God has blessed him abundantly. Satan challenges God that, if given permission to punish the man, Job will turn and curse God. God allows Satan to torment Job to test this bold claim, but he forbids Satan to take Job's life in the process.

In the course of one day, Job receives four messages, each bearing separate news that his livestock, servants, and ten children have all died due to marauding invaders or natural catastrophes. Job tears his clothes and shaves his head in mourning, but he still blesses God in his prayers. Satan appears in heaven again, and God grants him another chance to test Job. This time, Job is afflicted with horrible skin sores. His wife encourages him to curse God and to give up and die, but Job refuses, struggling to accept his circumstances.

Three of Job's friends, Eliphaz, Bildad, and Zophar, come to visit him, sitting with Job in silence for seven days out of respect for his mourning. On the seventh day, Job speaks, beginning a conversation in which each of the four men shares his thoughts on Job's afflictions in long, poetic statements.

Job curses the day he was born, comparing life and death to light and darkness. He wishes that his birth had been shrouded in darkness and longs to have never been born, feeling that light, or life, only intensifies his misery. Eliphaz responds that Job, who has comforted other people, now shows that he never really understood their pain. Eliphaz believes that Job's agony must be due to some sin Job has committed, and he urges Job to seek God's favor. Bildad and Zophar agree that Job must have committed evil to offend God's justice and argue that he should strive to exhibit more blameless behavior. Bildad surmises that Job's children brought their deaths upon themselves. Even worse, Zophar implies that whatever wrong Job has done probably deserves greater punishment than what he has received.

Job responds to each of these remarks, growing so irritated that he calls his friends "worthless physicians" who "whitewash [their advice] with lies" (13:4). After making pains to assert his blameless character, Job ponders man's relationship to God. He wonders why God judges' people by their actions if God can just as easily alter or forgive their behavior. It is also unclear to Job how a human can appease or court God's justice. God is unseen, and his ways are inscrutable and beyond human understanding. Moreover, humans cannot possibly persuade God with their words. God cannot be deceived, and Job admits that he does not even understand himself well enough to effectively plead his case to God. Job wishes for someone who can mediate between himself and God, or for God to send him to Sheol, the deep place of the dead.

Job's friends are offended that he scorns their wisdom. They think his questions are crafty and lack an appropriate fear of God, and they use many analogies and metaphors to stress their ongoing point that nothing good comes of wickedness. Job sustains his confidence in spite of these criticisms, responding that even if he has done evil, it is his own personal problem. Furthermore, he believes that there is a "witness" or a "Redeemer" in heaven who will vouch for his innocence (16:19, 19:25). After a while, the up-braiding proves too much for Job, and he grows sar-castic, impatient, and afraid. He laments the injus-tice that God lets wicked people prosper while he and countless other innocent people suffer. Job wants to confront God and complain, but he cannot physically find God to do it. He feels that wisdom is hidden from human minds, but he resolves to persist in pursuing wisdom by fearing God and avoiding evil.

Without provocation, another friend, Elihu, sud-denly enters the conversation. The young Elihu be-lieves that Job has spent too much energy vindicating himself rather than God. Elihu explains to Job that God communicates with humans by two ways—vi-sions and physical pain. He says that physical suffer-ing provides the sufferer with an opportunity to real-ize God's love and forgiveness when he is well again, understanding that God has "ransomed" him from an impending death (33:24). Elihu also assumes that Job must be wicked to be suffering as he is, and he thinks that Job's excessive talking is an act of rebel-lion against God.

God finally interrupts, calling from a whirlwind and demanding Job to be brave and respond to his questions. God's questions are rhetorical, intend-ing to show how little Job knows about creation and how much power God alone has. God describes many detailed aspects of his creation, praising especially his creation of two large beasts, the Behemoth and Leviathan. Overwhelmed by the encounter, Job acknowledges God's unlimited power and admits the limitations of his human knowledge. This response pleases God, but he is upset with Eliphaz, Bildad, and Zophar for spouting poor and theologically unsound advice. Job intercedes on their behalf, and God forgives them. God returns Job's health, providing him with twice as much property as before, new children, and an extremely long life.

ANALYSIS

The Book of Job is one of the most celebrated pieces of biblical literature, not only because it explores some of the most profound questions humans ask about their lives, but also because it is extremely well written. The work combines two literary forms, framing forty chapters of verse between two and a half chapters of prose at the beginning and the end. The poetic discourse of Job and his friends is unique in its own right. The lengthy conversation has the unified voice and consistent style of poetry, but it is a dialogue between characters who alter their moods, question their motives, change their minds, and undercut each other with sarcasm and innuendo. Although Job comes closest to doing so, no single character articulates one true or authoritative opinion. Each speaker has his own flaws as well as his own lofty moments of observation or astute theological insight."[16]

I will make you exceedingly fruitful, and I will make you into nations, and kings shall come from you. And I will establish my covenant between me and you and your offspring after you throughout their generations for an everlasting covenant, to be God to you and to your offspring after you. And I will give to you and to your offspring after you the land of your sojournings, all the land of Canaan, for an everlasting possession, and I will be their God.

Genesis 17:6-8, ESV

7

Boundaries

Brothers, if anyone is caught in any sin, you who are spiritual [that is, you who are responsive to the guidance of the Spirit] are to restore such a person in a spirit of gentleness [not with a sense of superiority or self-righteousness], keeping a watchful eye on yourself, so that you are not tempted as well. Carry one another's burdens and in this way you will fulfill the requirements of the law of Christ [that is, the law of Christian love]. For if anyone thinks he is something [special] when [in fact] he is nothing [special except in his own eyes], he deceives himself. But each one must carefully scrutinize his own work [examining his actions, attitudes, and behavior], and then he can have the personal satisfaction and inner joy of doing something commendable [a]without comparing himself to another. For every person will have to bear [with patience] his own burden [of faults and shortcomings for which he alone is responsible].

Galatians 6:1-5, AMP

BOUNDARIES IN DATING

This topic I wish I learned much earlier in life.

"What are boundaries? Personal boundaries are guidelines, rules or limits that a person creates to identify reasonable, safe and permissible ways for other people to behave toward them and how they will respond when someone passes those limits."

Establishing healthy boundaries in a relationship allows both partners to feel comfortable and develop positive self-esteem. In order to establish boundaries, you need to be clear with your partner who you are, what you want, your beliefs and values, and your limits.[17]

Let's talk about boundaries. I did everything backward with my life. If I knew what I know today I could have prevented so much heartache and pain in my life and others that were in my path. This one I struggled with a lot. I didn't have any boundaries in my home growing up, so this was a new behavior I needed to learn.

My boundaries were broken very early in life when my grandfather molested me. That set the precedent in my life from that day forward. Once this was established in my brain at a young age I didn't know what was healthy any longer. My thoughts at the time were, *If a loved one can do this to me, what else can be done from men later in my life?* Trust was broken. I didn't trust any longer after I was exposed to this horrific pain. The safety I once felt was destroyed and non-existent. This led to a long list of emotional traumas in me that made it difficult to identify what healthy connections with others looked like.

When I was violated and betrayed by my loved one my eternal pain grew heavy with fear and stress that weighed more in my soul where it was hard to engage interpersonal relationships. My judgment was wrong from that day forward. My poor judgment showed in the instability of relationships, promiscuity, sexual curiosity, lack of respect for my body, carelessness and no boundaries for myself with boys I dated.

The word "no" was a very hard word for me to say to people. I am a people-pleaser. I hate disappointing others. In relationships in the past I didn't want to be intimate with my partner, but I felt if I didn't, they would leave me. I hate feeling abandoned. The majority of my childhood that was one thing I constantly felt: I was deprived of love, safety, reassurance, peace, encouragement, and motivation to enjoy life.

> And since you know that he cares, let your language show it. Don't add words like "I swear to God" to your own words. Don't show your impatience by concocting oaths to hurry up God. Just say yes or no. Just say what is true. That way, your language can't be used against you.
>
> James 5:12, MSG

Being a people-pleaser had negative effects on my life. I was easily influenced or manipulated to do something that my heart knew wasn't right, but I worried about the outcome of displeasing the individual. It was hard for me to take a leap of faith with my actions while committing to a firm answer to stand my ground. This led to a litany of problems by becoming an easy target to be persuaded in the wrong direction because of my vulnerability.

I struggled with this 100% of the time. I saw so much inexcusable, criminal, shameful, and blameworthy behavior of sin that the thought of offending someone hurt my soul. I was tired of seeing disappointment in other peoples' eyes, so I wanted to do anything in my power to avoid hurting others. This led to a very bad habit of becoming a compulsive liar to avoid hurting other's feelings. I was frightened by the outcome so I would cover my tracks to avoid being caught in lies and avoid judgment of others.

Sometimes I was such a good liar I would start to believe my own lie, which caused my fantasy life to be woven into hybrid reality of the truth. This is how bad my thought process was in my late teens and early twenties. I looked up behaviors of people who tend to lie more than the fair share of people. This explains my mind at that time in my life. If someone you know, or you, have possibly experienced these types of behavior, don't be afraid to talk to someone about it so you can get help to overcome it and live a healthier life.

The Behavior of a Compulsive Liar

"The difference between an average person's lying behavior and a compulsive liar are the reasons for their lies. When a person with no mental health issues lies, they usually have a specific purpose in mind for lying. They might be trying to hide an affair and lie to their spouse or try to get ahead at their job by lying to their boss.

Compulsive liars are not necessarily trying to manipulate others or achieve anything by their incessant lying behavior. A compulsive liar seems to lie regardless of what the situation is and for seemingly no reason at all. Their lying becomes a habit and is second nature to them in a way that they can no longer control.

For someone with an issue of compulsive lying, their need to bend and stretch the truth becomes comforting to them. Being honest can feel difficult and uncomfortable and they feel much more at ease making up false information. This feeling of comfort they feel when lying can become addictive because it makes them feel safe and impels them to lie even more.

When a compulsive liar makes up a lie it can often be believable because it has some truthful elements to it. The lies that they tell tend to show them in a positive light or elicit sympathy and attention from others. Their lies they tell are sometimes a way for them to create a different persona or get people to notice them.

Personality Disorders and Compulsive Lying

As part of the underlying personality disorder that causes them to lie, many compulsive liars have serious issues with self-esteem. They make up lies that show them in a positive light because they are uncomfortable with their true selves and feel that they aren't good enough or worthy. They might lie to appear more interesting or admirable to people who may be completely unaware that their statements are untrue.

People with issues like borderline personality disorder may lie constantly because they want to avoid feelings of shame. They feel incredibly intense emotions and their lying habit may help alleviate some of their feelings of low self-esteem, shame and weakness. They might lie to cover up aspects of their personality or mistakes that they are embarrassed about.

Compulsive liars with personality disorders are also lying because they have impulsive behavior that they can't control. People with borderline personality disorder tend to do things without thinking about the consequences and their impulsiveness can cause a lot of problems for them. They may lie simply because they are not thinking, and they naturally respond with lies instead of speaking honestly.

People with narcissistic personality disorder often lie because they have a highly developed false self. They may lie to make themselves appear smarter or more superior than others so that they can hide any weakness. Narcissists want to make others feel less than them and they may lie as a way to make others believe that they are inferior.

Different disorders may lead to various lying habits but ultimately a compulsive liar chooses to lie because they have a compulsive need to cover up their true self. Their lying behavior always has internal motives rather than an external reason. However, the more often they lie the more their behavior is going to have an impact on their career, their relationships and their family.

Anyone with an issue of compulsive lying can learn to change their behavior if they receive a diagnosis for their underlying personality disorder and professional treatment. If you or someone you know compulsively lies, then contact a mental health professional for help [18]

What this adds up to, then, is this: no more lies, no more pretense. Tell your neighbor the truth. In Christ's body we're all connected to each other, after all. When you lie to others, you end up lying to yourself.

Ephesians 4:25, MSG

As I was getting older, I saw from my own eyes that my parents didn't have boundaries within their marriage. Their marriage was broken. They didn't respect each other. There were no rules or limits created among themselves so the marriage was destroyed by abuse, alcohol, and adultery. My father went past those limits more often than I could count. When my mother and father fought, it led to hitting each other and vulgar language that was spoken negative and hurtful. My mother would cry all the time because she felt belittled, unloved, treated disrespectful. Her self-esteem was destroyed by all the fighting and cutthroat words that were spoken to her that was damaging to her spirit. There was no true love and respect for each other. There was no gentleness between them. There was only hate that festered up. Their marriage represented a burning volcano that was about to erupt and anything that crossed the hot lava would be destroyed in the process, which was myself, my siblings, and my cousins; the innocent bystanders in the cross hairs of the explosion.

There was no happy medium with my parents. They crossed the line throughout their marriage along with no consistency in parenting. In our home there were no rules to follow or guidance to direct us children to know right from wrong. We didn't have a mentor for us to model learn how our behavior should be or actions to adhere by.

When there are no boundaries in a child's life it can have long-term impacts on their growth, especially when a child is neglected emotionally. This causes adverse effects in the child's brain development such as a lack of emotional attachment to others, or the fear of rejection of their needs. Children are naturally curious and have a playful spirit. When their attentions are being ignored or not being nurtured by their parents or caregiver with love, this can create insecurity internally where a child will drift away and stop caring or trying to please others for the fear of being shamed or humiliated by the neglect of the parent/caregiver. If their feelings are being minimized it causes pain in the child's soul where they lose joy and laughter. They become more serious and put up walls to protect their feelings and avoid being hurt. This is what happened to me.

Every day my wall went up more and more. The joy was sucked out of me. I used to love playing and having fun with my friends but that started to drift away in my soul because of the lack of nurturing I had from my parents. I was always on guard to protect myself from being hurt, and protect my siblings and cousins so I developed a more serious role. My laughter started to wither away slowly each day and it was extremely hard to laugh at people's jokes. When I had sleepovers with my friends, everybody would be laughing and enjoying their time and I remember having to force a smile on my face and fake laughter so no one would know the pain I felt inside. I had a difficult time trying to dig the laughter out of me. It was not a natural feeling for me like it was for most people in this world that grew up in a loving and safe home filled with joy.

It was nice to have breaks from my house. I was relieved to not be at home dealing with the misery of my parents, but the sadness was still in my soul. With all the trauma I experienced it forced me to go into survival mode because I was not being taken care of and left to fend for myself. I didn't have the luxury of being a child, I had to grow up fast to just survive. Even though my maturity level was still a child, it led me to grow up more quickly than my other friends because of the circumstances and lack of resources that were given to me. My quench of thirst longed to have water to fill my body because I was so dehydrated and exhausted in my journey that my well became drained eventually it dried out.

The way I fed the numbness and dehydration of by body was to seek attention from boys, experience drugs and alcohol, and become sexually active at the young age of thirteen just to feel loved and wanted. I wanted to have some power and control in my life. As my child mind was thinking, *Why not? If no one was going to reach out to care for me or to show me love I'd find other means to get that emotion filled.* The consequences from my actions were overwhelming. I disconnected my feelings because it was only making me hurt worse when I got upset. I learned to turn that emotion off when needed to.

Imagine yourself as a young child watching your parents' fight unfold right in front of your very own eyes. You see them yelling, hitting each other, and drinking. The sadness weighs heavily on your soul because there is nothing you can do to stop the abuse from happening but cry and beg them to stop hurting each other. This is traumatizing for a child to experience. No child should ever be put in this predicament but so many children are. It saddens my soul.

That is why I want to fight for the innocent children and teens who also had this horrific experience that I endured. These precious souls need the love that they truly deserve. Every beloved child of God should know how it feels to be wanted, loved, and nurtured from their loved one. They should be recognized from the pure angelic spirit that was given to them by God when they were born. Many neglected children don't receive empathy from their parents. These kids are craving to be noticed. Instead they are mistreated and abused. There is no element of peace nor form of care regarding their emotional wellbeing.

As parents, we should establish routines for our children along with modeling healthy behavior in front of them. The way we can do this is to allow our children to be creative, build confidence in them, teach them skills to learn to overcome adversity when disappointment comes their way by facing their fears with loving support, be patient and not rush, nurture the growth of their minds, build them back up emotionally when setbacks arise, teach them to trust in themselves, teach them problem solving, let them talk and express the problems they want to share, and encourage them to understand the "how" and "why" when facing tough decisions.

What I have learned about resilience for a child is that we need to encourage them to bounce back from stress. When we do this, we can help the child to become more brave, to be curious to learn new things, and want to be able to use their skills to help others in life. We can also give them the hope to believe in themselves, knowing anything they try they can achieve by faith, God's grace, and direction. We must help our children to find their purpose in life.

We are pressed on every side by troubles, but we are
not crushed. We are perplexed, but not driven to despair. We are hunted down, but never abandoned by
God. We get knocked down, but we are not destroyed.

2 Corinthians 4:8-9, NLT

In order for my life to change, one thing I needed to learn
was boundaries. I went to counseling to get help with this. I
was introduced to a book called, *Boundaries: When to Say Yes,
How to Say No to Take Control of Your Life*, by Dr. Henry Cloud and
Dr. John Townsend. This was the beginning of my journey to be
set free from being controlled by others. I needed help learning
to make healthy boundaries for myself to grow my walk with
God. This changed my life and it freed me from regret for feeling guilty when I stuck up for myself and said no when it was
needed. I was no longer feeling convicted separating myself
from others that it was a hindrance to my walk with Christ. I
embraced the new freedom I felt. Every day it was becoming
easier to set limits and distinguish when I felt the Holy Spirit
speak to me when things weren't right. I was able to recognize
when I was being manipulated. I was able to be stronger and
walk away.

I needed to work on and overcome co-dependency, set
boundaries that I could obtain for myself, and break my perfectionist spirit. Co-dependent children who grew up in an
alcoholic home, or had a dysfunctional family like me have circumstances that can cause negative emotional behavior. This
learned behavior can get passed down from one generation to

another. Children who live in this type of environment can suffer from fear, anger, pain, and shame when being ignored or denied the attention they need. As a result of their emotions being disregarded they become "survivors". Some children will develop compulsive behaviors later in their adulthood, like workaholism, to prove their self-worth. The co-dependent may have good intentions, but they try to take too much on in a caretaker role becoming a martyr. They put their needs last to try to better the situation they are in. They lose themselves in a role by taking care of others and their own desires are put on a back burner.

CHARACTERISTICS OF CO-DEPENDENT PEOPLE ARE:

- An exaggerated sense of responsibility for the actions of others
- A tendency to confuse love and pity, with the tendency to "love" people they can pity and rescue
- A tendency to do more than their share, all of the time
- A tendency to become hurt when people don't recognize their efforts
- An unhealthy dependence on relationships. The co-dependent will do anything to hold on to a relationship; to avoid the feeling of abandonment
- An extreme need for approval and recognition
- A sense of guilt when asserting themselves

- A compelling need to control others
- Lack of trust in self and/or others
- Fear of being abandoned or alone
- Difficulty identifying feelings
- Rigidity/difficulty adjusting to change
- Problems with intimacy/boundaries
- Chronic anger
- Lying/dishonesty
- Poor communications
- Difficulty making decisions

QUESTIONNAIRE TO IDENTIFY SIGNS OF CO-DEPENDENCY

This condition appears to run in different degrees, whereby the intensity of symptoms is on a spectrum of severity, as opposed to an all or nothing scale. Please note that only a qualified professional can make a diagnosis of co-dependency; not everyone experiencing these symptoms suffers from co-dependency.

1. Do you keep quiet to avoid arguments?
2. Are you always worried about others' opinions of you?
3. Have you ever lived with someone with an alcohol or drug problem?
4. Have you ever lived with someone who hits or belittles you?
5. Are the opinions of others more important than your own?

6. Do you have difficulty adjusting to changes at work or home?

7. Do you feel rejected when significant others spend time with friends?

8. Do you doubt your ability to be who you want to be?

9. Are you uncomfortable expressing your true feelings to others?

10. Have you ever felt inadequate?

11. Do you feel like a "bad person" when you make a mistake?

12. Do you have difficulty taking compliments or gifts?

13. Do you feel humiliation when your child or spouse makes a mistake?

14. Do you think people in your life would go downhill without your constant efforts?

15. Do you frequently wish someone could help you get things done?

16. Do you have difficulty talking to people in authority, such as the police or your boss?

17. Are you confused about who you are or where you are going with your life?

18. Do you have trouble saying "no" when asked for help?

19. Do you have trouble asking for help?

20. Do you have so many things going at once that you can't do justice to any of them?

If you identify with several of these symptoms; are dissatisfied with yourself or your relationships; you should consider seeking professional help. Arrange for a diagnostic evaluation with a licensed physician or psychologist experienced in treating co-dependency.[19]

After reading these characteristics and signs of co-dependency I have seen what I have done firsthand in the past which caused many problems with my growth.

As an abused child, growing up I struggled to have any control of my life. I constantly needed to be perfect in everything I did. I felt if I tried to be the best, I could control my own destiny and prevent pain and heartache in my life. By doing this I caused more pain in my soul of the unrealistic high expectations I held to myself and others around me. I did this with my work. The harder I worked and the longer hours I put in made me feel like I could provide a lifestyle for myself that was comfortable to avoid lacking money to take care of myself and put food on the table.

I had a huge fear that if I didn't work, I would end up like my parents who was poor and had a miserable life. I didn't want to turn out like them so my fear took over and I did everything I could to control my environment to feel safe and secure. I had no one to fall back on if I needed help with my bills because my family didn't have the money to take care of me. I couldn't depend on them, only myself. This created a lot of pressure and stress on myself to survive. I am a planner. If I don't plan what

I need to do I feel out of control and off balance. It's a sense of security for me to have peace and no anxiety by preparing ahead of time.

I am very hard on myself. Being raised by neglectful parents I tended to be harder on myself and more susceptible to abusive relationships. If I made a mistake, I was so critical of myself. When things would fall apart, I would blame myself that I was the problem. I especially did this when I was older and dating. I thought there was something wrong with me because my relationships would fall apart, and I was treated poorly with verbal abuse. I struggled learning to trust myself to make healthy decisions. I needed the constant validation because I was not validated as a child. I sought out the wrong kind of attention that was harmful to my growth.

I had destructive behavior. If I didn't get what I needed in the relationship I would sabotage it. I was willing to do anything I could to get the approval I needed. If I didn't get my needs met, and if I was brushed away from my hurts, I would act out in the relationship by rebelling to get noticed. This was someone who was trying to reach out for help and was desperate for attention.

I started to get a handle of my emotions by seeking counseling and taking classes with other abused people to develop the healthy skills to cope when faced with these situations. I would be able to handle it much better.

I started to equip myself by journaling my feelings on paper. This allowed me to acknowledge my hurts and trace the source of why I felt the way I did so I could get a hold of my feelings.

I learned to be less reactive by getting to know myself more intimately with Jesus. I started to recognize my patterns and what was triggering these emotions or outbursts. I made time for complete silence by having my daily quiet time with God, reading my Bible, and learning His word. I embraced guidance from other women in Bible studies to be coached, and allowed them to invest time in me by being vulnerable and seeking the direction of these women of God who had a strong foundation in their relationship with Jesus.

I stopped criticizing myself and learned to love me. I embraced my unique qualities that God gave me. I stopped judging my past failures and learned to turn them into good by helping others were in the same boat as me. I learned I am perfect in the eyes of Jesus and He has forgiven me for all the terrible sins I have done. I decided to not dread on the past any longer by appreciating my flaws and my sinful behavior in the past. I owned my faults. I started to work on developing myself by reading self-help books, going to church on a regular basis, and surrounding myself with people who followed Jesus. I started to enjoy life instead of always looking through a negative lens.

My God is bigger than my hurricanes. He has taught me to solidify my old patterns by breaking them down one by one. He brought a new identity in me as a child of God who is loved, treasured, and valued by being his little princess that He honors and respects. He taught me to respect myself and not let anyone come in and disrespect me. He gave me a new vision through Him that I would not distort my vision by perceiving I am the problem, but I am a solution to go help others who experienced the same trauma that knocked on my door. God taught me that instead of sweeping my feelings under a rug, to bring my pain to Him and He will heal my soul and bring the newfound confidence I needed from His power of love that is everlasting.

He gave me dreams of my future to help express my story for others. I want all people to find the resurrection of Jesus in their life like I have. He has given me new dreams. He took my old memories away that were holding me captive. He gave me encouragement to not let my mistakes paralyze me any longer. He breathed life back into me that I once had as a toddler. God carried me to shore, saved my life, and gave me purpose again.

Take a leap of faith and just do it. You won't regret stepping out and grabbing a hold of Jesus' hand. Our heavenly Father will not fail you like our earthly father can. He will restore your soul.

Embrace your failures and become the teacher. Our lives are our testimonies. We are not here on earth for our own selfishness. We are here to live a fuller life by encouraging, bringing compassion, and sharing wisdom for others to find fuller lives with God's love and protection. We are here to escort people to find Jesus as their Lord and Savior. Many years we have hardwired our mind with the wrong beliefs and incorrect thinking patterns that cloud our judgment. The devil may have stolen our joy for some time and told us lies, but we don't have to let him win any longer. Let's bring purpose to lost and innocent souls.

We all have messy lives. Don't let that mess keep you from experiencing the beauty of God's creation in heaven. He is here to redefine us and bring insight to what has plagued us. He is polishing our souls for the next chapter in our lives. Let's break free from the chains and bring more laughter to our souls. We must stop imprisoning our souls and allowing the torment to isolate our thought process. Let's agree to not let the enemy win and hide behind a mask because we are too ashamed of what we have done. Stop worrying about the mistakes you have made. Instead move forward with a newfound energy and excitement for what lies ahead on the journey that God has given to you.

> For here's what I'm going to do: I'm going to take you out of these countries, gather you from all over, and bring you back to your own land. I'll pour pure water over you and scrub you clean. I'll give you a new heart, put a new spirit in you. I'll remove the stone heart from your body and replace it with a heart that's God-willed, not self-willed. I'll put my Spirit in you and make it possible for you to do what I tell you and live by my commands. You'll once again live in the land I gave your ancestors. You'll be my people! I'll be your God!
>
> Ezekiel 36:24-28, MSG

BOUNDARIES ON DATING

We must ask ourselves what is too far in the physical aspect in our relationships? This part for me I did not know. Earlier in my life that boundary was broken so I didn't understand the concept of what true boundaries looked like. I struggled with the same guilt one after another in my relationships. I couldn't believe I allowed myself to go that far in the relationship. Even though my heart knew better, it was so hard for me to say no.

Little by little as I was dating, I gained more confidence to speak up in the relationship and explain to them the importance of wanting to save myself for marriage. I didn't want to be intimate any longer. I knew I wasn't pure and innocent, that I had already had sex before marriage. I wanted to live a better path and hold myself more accountable. I may not have respected myself in the past, but I was working hard to love myself and respect my body by establishing boundaries. I knew Jesus saw more in me and I wanted to see that in myself. Did I slip and make mistakes? Absolutely. I would give in, then feel so guilty about what I had done. I tried to take it one day at a time.

The more I dug into my counseling and fed my spirit with the new kind of thinking it started to sink in my mind. It took a lot of practice. I was stuck in a cycle of the repetitive struggle of going too far. My guilt and shame would overtake me at times. I was so hard on myself. I couldn't understand why this was hard for me to overcome. I had many deep-rooted dysfunctional thinking from years of bad behavior. I would lose my will power in the heat of the moment. Only Jesus could free me from this cycle. Here are some suggestions that I learned through my mistakes in dating. God can redeem anyone.

> Each time he said, "My grace is all you need. My power works best in weakness." So now I am glad to boast about my weaknesses, so that the power of Christ can work through me.
>
> 2 Corinthians 12:9, NLT

1. Have someone who shares the same beliefs as you.
2. Talk about it ahead of time when you start dating someone what the expectations are.
3. Never be alone with the person in their room to cause temptation.
4. Plan your dates in public places to prevent yourself making poor decisions in the heat of the moment.
5. Set boundaries physically what you feel is too far to not tempt each other
6. Do double dates to hold yourself accountable from temptation.
7. If the relationship gets serious, don't move in together before marriage. Live separately to prevent sexual temptation no matter how much you love each other.
8. Be careful what you wear in front of your partner to prevent sexual arousal for them.

9. Avoid pornography and social media temptation.

10. Recognize your weaknesses and vulnerabilities ahead of time so you can avoid falling into the trap of your enemy, luring you to do make a bad choice to fill that void that is missing to feel whole or complete emotionally.

I started to recognize these boundaries and implemented them in my daily life. I was using these tools to help guide me to heal and learn to grow to love myself. When I was least expecting to be in a relationship, I met an amazing man who now is my sweet husband. I met him on Myspace. I was led for some reason to send him a private email thanking him for his service for our country. He emailed me back so appreciative of a young woman being so thoughtful about him serving and fighting for our country. He was used to getting compliments from older adults but not from someone our age. We would chat and have mature conversations online. Then we agreed to meet.

When we met for the first time, we hung out in a public area where we worked out together at his gym at his apartment complex, but our true first date was at church. We set our boundaries ahead of time to keep us from being tempted. I may not have been perfect when I met him, nor was he perfect. But he understood the importance to stay pure in our relationship. We fell in love with each other so quickly when we both least expected to be in a relationship. We got married and have been married for twelve years. I have never been happier.

Has it been easy? No. However, every hurdle in our marriage has been worth it. I would never take away all the ups and downs we went through in our marriage. I still have things to work through within myself from the damage in my life, but he has been my rock, by my side encouraging me every step of the way. God has given my husband the needed patience and abundant amount of love by allowing his heart to be open to understand me with all the insecurities and struggles that I needed to overcome.

Here is a chart for guidance with healthy and unhealthy aspects in relationships. I saw this chart for setting boundaries in your relationship on a blog I was reading.[20]

HEALTHY	UNHEALTHY
Feeling responsible for your own happiness	Feeling incomplete without your partner
Friendships exist outside of the relationship	Relying on your partner for happiness
Open and honest communication	Game-playing or manipulation
Respecting differences in your partner	Jealousy
Asking honestly what is wanted	Feeling unable to express what is wanted
Accepting endings	Unable to let go

BOUNDARIES IN MARRIAGE

From the beginning of our marriage we agreed not to speak about our past relationships nor anything sexually we may have done. We wanted to set a tone in our relationship that was going to be different than what we had done in the past. In my husband's eyes he sees me pure, and that he has been the only person in my life that I have been with. He didn't want to taint anything in his mind or get bad images of things that he and I have done in the past. We wanted to start fresh and clean like we were the first people we had ever been with. He doesn't know to this day all the bad decisions I have made.

One thing we have done was agree to never be alone with the opposite sex to prevent the temptation of adultery. We agreed to not speak to our former relationship partners to help us not to be accessible to unwanted feelings that could cause confusion or doubt in our marriage. Have I made it easy for my husband at times? No.

We set boundaries when we go to the doctors to only see the same sex; we are to avoid any temptation of lust. We built trust in our marriage from the beginning. We were always open, letting each other know when we went somewhere so we know our spouse is safe from harm's way. We wanted to bring comfort in all areas we could in our marriage. It may seem like we were trying to be in control of each other in our marriage, but we were bringing safety and peace to never question or waiver in our love for one another.

A few more things we agreed on were to never leave the house when arguing and never go to bed angry. We wanted to build a strong foundation of marriage where we never doubted our love or attentions for each other. God has been the center of our marriage. We have done the *Love & Respect Bible Study* by Emerson Eggerichs, Ph.D., attended marriage teachings at church conferences, and a marriage retreat when we first got married; attend small Bible study groups with other married couples; have date nights (which is super important in your marriage). We have also taken trips together just him and I. Now that our kids are older we can leave them with family members or babysitters and go refresh our marriage. Lastly, I have read tons of marriage and self-help books to try to soak up as much as I could to retrain my thought process.

It hasn't always been rainbows and butterflies, nor are we perfect. I struggled with intimacy in our marriage. When I learned to set boundaries for myself, I cut off that old life of mine that was impure and it was hard to allow myself to be open freely and intimately with my husband. I was scared to death if I allowed certain feelings inside me to surface that I would bring the wrong person out of me like I was in the past. I was desperate to be a different person this time. I wanted to avoid all cause of temptation for me so I would never cheat on my husband. When I did this, I blocked certain sexual feelings that I once had and was not able to find the security to be completely open with my husband.

Throughout my life I was always in relationships where men wanted or needed something from me, along with taking my childlike innocence. When we got married I felt like I didn't have to have sex to get the love I needed from my husband. I finally was with someone who loved and cared for me so profoundly that it was the purest love that God gave us. I didn't feel like I needed to give him sex to feel whole. However, when I did this, I hurt our marriage by not allowing myself to be open intimately with him. He thought I wasn't attracted to him and he felt unloved at times because I wasn't showing him affection with my love for him in a more intimate or physical touch.

My husband's love language is touch. When I wasn't providing this to him it started to cause doubt in him in our marriage. He thought maybe he made a mistake marrying me. This was a work in progress. This almost cost our marriage. I was more determined than ever to fight for our marriage. I fought tooth and nail to save our marriage with lots of prayer, encouragement from wonderful friends and caring loved ones that were in our life, along with showing proof to my husband that he was worth fighting for. I wasn't going to give up without a fight and showed him my love was real for him. I needed to give my husband reassurance that he meant the whole world to me.

Don't take life for granted. Take hold of your marriages and hold them tight. Fight for your spouse. When rough times come you show them how they are loved, honored, and cherished. Let them know you are by their side through thick and thin. Always tell your spouse how nice they look. Compliment them how much you are grateful for their love for you, and appreciate all the things they do.

Make them feel special. If you let that love die it can destroy your soul along with causing unwanted insecurities that you both never had before. Sometimes we must break walls down that have guarded and protected our hearts for so long to avoid pain, fear, or abandonment. This brings more hurt and harm than good. Hold onto those precious moments because you don't know when they will be gone. I learned a hard lesson in life by taking advantage of my marriage and floating by on autopilot. I put things first before my spouse and gave him my leftovers. I almost lost my best friend and the love of my life because of my fears.

Squeeze hold of your spouse and listen to the warning signs when they are trying to tell you what is bothering them in your marriage. Try to be the best you can be for them even when you don't feel up to it or are too tired to put the effort in it. It's not worth the pain of losing your spouse because you don't want to give in to things that your spouse needs or wants. Pay attention to their love language. It may not be the same as yours, but you must put in every effort you can to meet their needs as they will return that to you. Cuddle with your spouse. Stop what you are doing on the phone if it consumes you. Lift your head up and look at them. Turn off all electronics and give your spouse 100% attention because they deserve all of you not half of you.

We must treat our spouses like Kings and Queens. We are God's prince and princess and He adores us so we must do the same for our spouse. Remember to slow down and be present with your spouse. We must pause long enough for our spouse to resonate all of us so both of you can be in the moment of your marriage. Our marriage from God is held to a higher standard. God intends for us to be one with our spouse the way we are intended to be in one with Christ.

> However, each man among you [without exception] is to love his wife as his very own self [with behavior worthy of respect and esteem, always seeking the best for her with an attitude of lovingkindness], and the wife [must see to it] that she respects and delights in her husband [that she notices him and prefers him and treats him with loving concern, treasuring him, honoring him, and holding him dear].
>
> Ephesians 5:33 AMP

DESCRIPTION OF A WORTHY WOMAN

> An excellent woman [one who is spiritual, capable, intelligent, and virtuous], who is he who can find her? Her value is more precious than jewels *and* her worth is far above rubies *or* pearls. The heart of her husband trusts in her [with secure confidence], And he will have no lack of gain. She comforts, encourages, *and* does him only good and not evil All the days of her life.
>
> Proverbs 31:10-12, AMP

One of the greatest gifts God blessed me with was making me out of a man by taking a rib from man's own flesh to give me life to breathe. God gave me an amazing man to be a leader over my life and my children. He held my hand to keep me going through the tough times. He replicates God's strength. He is tough, honest, full of love; caring and trustworthy.

8

Affirmation

May He grant you out of the riches of His glory, to be strengthened and spiritually energized with power through His Spirit in your inner self, [indwelling your innermost being and personality], so that Christ may dwell in your hearts through your faith. And may you, having been [deeply] rooted and [securely] grounded in love, be fully capable of comprehending with all the saints (God's people) the width and length and height and depth of His love [fully experiencing that amazing, endless love]; and [that you may come] to know [practically, through personal experience] the love of Christ which far surpasses [mere] knowledge [without experience], that you may be filled up [throughout your being] to all the fullness of God [so that you may have the richest experience of God's presence in your lives, completely filled and flooded with God Himself].

Now to Him who is able to [carry out His purpose and] do superabundantly more than all that we dare ask or think [infinitely beyond our greatest prayers, hopes, or dreams], according to His power that is at work within us, to Him be the glory in the church and in Christ Jesus throughout all generations forever and ever. Amen.

Ephesians 3:16-21, AMP

TRANSFORMING YOUR MIND

We have a choice to make good or bad decisions by allowing what we choose to come into our thoughts daily. We must take action in our lives by developing faith that God will deliver us and break our bad habits. We must be willing to fail and keep choosing and exercising our minds to take the necessary steps to change. It takes constant effort and determination to keep pressing forward even when you don't feel like doing so.

God created us to go to battle and be warriors to fight for the weak. We must put on the shield of armor daily so we can allow God to fight off our enemies. God has set a journey for us to be brought back to life by restoring the original self back in us; to be better and become brand new with God's help. We need to flourish and release the past hurts. Don't rehearse the strongholds or pain you have endured. Pursue healing and pray for miracles that God will restore your soul. Feed your spirit with God's love and restoration. Repair what is broken in you.

What makes you feel happy or gives you energy? What do you want Jesus to do for you? We cannot live our lives the same way every day. We must do something different each day to make a change in our spirit. We need to change things in our lives and cut out what is bringing you down. See yourself through God's image of you by becoming confident and unshakeable. I had a lady in my Bible study who would say, "Have *Godfidence.*" I love this. This spoke to me when we did the *Fully Alive* Bible study by Susan Larson. Let's get rid of all your distractions. We must be open and cooperate with God to allow change to happen in our lives. Have you limited God in your life by your own unbelief?

> But without faith it is impossible to [walk with God and] please Him, for whoever comes [near] to God must [necessarily] believe that God exists and that He rewards those who [earnestly and diligently] seek Him.
>
> Hebrews 11:6, AMP

> So then, strengthen hands that are weak *and* knees that tremble. Cut through and make smooth, straight paths for your feet [that are safe and go in the right direction], so that *the leg* which is lame may not be put out of joint, but rather may be healed.
>
> Hebrews 12:12-13, AMP

> We have come to know [by personal observation and experience], and have believed [with deep, consistent faith] the love which God has for us. God is love, and

the one who abides in love abides in God, and God abides *continually* in him.

1 John 4:16 AMP

The life of God's rewards is everlasting love by the grace which He gives us. Don't bow down and be a fearful slave. We must share alongside with Jesus' suffering. Be of good cheer because Jesus overcame the devil by dying for us. We are a work in progress and God will call us out of our sin so we can confront it head on, get out of our comfort zone, and break free of our destructive behavior. God is working in our souls to encourage us to break free from constant disappointment and rehashing our losses or unfulfilled expectations. Our heartbreaks and disappointments are meant to inspire us to become passionate doers to help others along our journey. What negative thoughts does the devil speak to your soul that you know are not true? If your story is not good right now, then God is not done with you yet. We must be a better friend to ourselves.

My sweet friends don't stay discouraged. God is with us everywhere we go. Speak life to yourself. Scream at the top of your lungs that you are not "broken" but you are the child of the "Most High" that has given you the authority to have a fulfilled, abundant life. Speak truth that you are not shattered in millions of pieces. Don't question God's ability however long he takes. He is your Conqueror.

Speak God's truth in you by asking to see His will for your life. Ask God for help cleansing your soul and capturing the wrongdoing before you take a step in the enemy's trap. God will use your life as a testimony for the sheep to find God's glory through your life. God will bless your life as a faithful servant and keep you from living a destructive path. We must believe in ourselves that we can be better than what we were taught from dysfunctional thinking. Live your life as a testimony. Let's agree to rewrite your story.

There is a right season, time and purpose for each of our lives. If you listen to God's words carefully, He will keep His promise to protect you and your family. Listen carefully so we don't miss God's message. Make sure you are looking at the big picture instead of the little things, and start believing in God, and your life will be blessed. Be obedient to the Lord. Do not be frightened of the outcome. Step out of your comfort zone to pursue your happiness.

I had an incredible friend in my past who really helped and encouraged me to make the right decisions in my life. He showed me what love really is by God, not by men on earth. What I learned is that true love is patient, kind, not envious, or jealous, not prideful, not rude, not selfish, not angered but forgives, truthful and most of all believes in God that has hope, bears fruit, and endures (1 Cor 13:4-7).

> Love bears all things [regardless of what comes], believes all things [looking for the best in each one], hopes all things [remaining steadfast during difficult times], endures all things [without weakening].
>
> 1 Corinthians 13:7, AMP

In order for me to love anyone in my life, I needed to love myself first. I had to fully commit to making my life a priority by seeking God's healing instead of dating the wrong men. The constant cycle of abuse I put myself through over and over had to be stopped. My sweet caring friend was exactly what I needed at that time. He was an amazing friend that made me stand still long enough to direct me to a mirror and hold my head straight to make myself look at my reflection. Do you know how uncomfortable that is?

I didn't like who I saw in the mirror staring back at me. Who was this person? Was this person weak, abused, molested, raped, abandoned, defeated, and unloved? Or was she loved, wanted, strong, blessed, an overcomer and a conqueror? I decided from that day forward I would look at myself as beautifully and wonderfully made in God's image. This person sounds more exciting, enjoyable, full of life, and has a lot of love to give. This is someone who wants to make a difference in this world and help other abused kids, teens, and women young and old. This is my destiny.

My friend was uplifting me and spoke affirmations of kind words and held me accountable. He encouraged me to write down loving words about myself on paper and put them up all around my house on the mirrors so I could read them every time I saw a mirror. He told me to continue to repeat God's truth about who I am. The more I did this, the more I started to believe what I was saying about myself. Each day I was getting more encouraged and gained a newfound faith in myself that was ready for change to my soul.

My friend had a patient heart like God. He helped me to learn not to worry about being tempted by the world. He showed me how to reflect God's words out of my mouth by speaking positively, and that God could always turn a bad situation into good. When you are struggling in life and feel like you cannot get ahead of the fear, know that God is stronger than us and we should allow Him to take our hands and carry us out of the mess by facing it head on.

Two heads are stronger than one. The devil fears us when we are in God's Word and feeding our spirit life. The devil loses his grip on us when we have God's power around us. He cannot touch us when God is moving powerfully in us and His plan has set in motion. God was teaching me how to be a powerful, strong woman that won't falter, but stand my feet firm on the ground. He was teaching me not to be a pushover. He made me brave to fight and to conqueror our enemy better, giving me the skills I needed to let good win over evil.

God leads us away from situations where we are vulnerable and have the opportunity to sin. God does not tempt man, but allows man to be tested. God has promised to take care of us, but we have to follow His word if we want God's blessings in life. God will help us to resist from evil, help us to say no when confronted with what we know is wrong, and helps us to run away from temptations.

And do not lead us into temptation but deliver us from evil. [For Yours is the kingdom and the power and the glory forever. Amen.]

Matthew 6:13, AMP

Blessed [happy, spiritually prosperous, favored by God] is the man who is steadfast under trial *and* perseveres when tempted; for when he has passed the test *and* been approved, he will receive the [victor's] crown of life which *the Lord* has promised to those who love Him.

James 1:12, AMP

SELF-AFFIRMATION

Affirmation is an act of affirming one's own worthiness and value as an individual for beneficial effect, such as increasing one's confidence or raising self-esteem.

Speak out loud to yourself on a daily basis to help you to start believing in yourself for change.

1. I am a Child of God.
2. I am worthy to be loved and wanted.
3. I love who I am in the eyes of God.
4. I resonate God's beauty.
5. My life has a purpose, to inspire others.
6. I believe in myself; that I am a leader and have a calling in life.

7. I am destined to do great things in my journey.
8. I have a gift to encourage others in life to find hope and peace.
9. I am smart, able, and competent.
10. I am a strong, determined overcomer and fierce person.

We must rewire our brains to speak to our subconscious minds, by ingraining our thought process with positive words instead of negative thinking. When we hold negative thoughts in our mind for a long period of time it will manifest into something dangerous that can overpower you to make bad decisions. Think about when you allow those thoughts to cultivate you with fear. It can become overwhelming, your stomach will feel like it's in knots, or acid burning the lining in your belly that can make you become sick or hospitalized. The more you allow that to overtake your healthy thinking the more frequently you will become sick. That it is a vicious cycle of never-ending stress that takes all the good feelings you once had and replaces them with negative thoughts. We need to learn how to speak more positively to ourselves. When we give ourselves the right tools we will allow powerful change of healing in our body, mind, heart and spirit.

I found some other things helpful for me. I would write down scriptures on a 3x5 card and put them next to my desk at work. I would read them out loud and practice memorizing them so that when I had a bad day, I could quote that scripture out loud to myself to give me the strength to get me through the day. When you develop a routine to speak to your soul with constant prayer it will help your spirit to grow more mature. When you have the discipline, you will find yourself developing a deeper relationship with God, and your faith will sprout with the greater desire to care for yourself and the temple of your body that was given to you for the Holy Spirit to work through you.

> Do you not know *and* understand that you [the church] are the temple of God, and that the Spirit of God dwells [permanently] in you [collectively and individually]?
>
> 1 Corinthians 3:16, AMP

Please review these items below for helpful tips that you can speak to yourself. Read through them and choose something that you need encouragement with that speaks to your soul. I found this a great read from Dr. Jonathan Parker.

GOD AFFIRMATIONS
- I acknowledge God in all creation.
- I love God and God loves me.
- I surrender my life to divine will.
- I feel the deep peace of God.
- I ask God's angels to surround me with light.
- I allow God to work through me.
- I am open and receive God's guidance.
- I feel God in my heart.

- I surrender into the arms of God.
- God lives in me and through me.

BLESSINGS AFFIRMATIONS

- I am worthy and open to receive blessings.
- My life is a blessing to others.
- My days are filled with blessings.
- I bless everyone I meet today.
- I feel blessed today.

TRUST AFFIRMATIONS

- I trust my life is divinely guided.
- I trust the outcomes in my life are for the best.
- I trust that all that I need comes to me when needed.
- I feel safe trusting God in my life.
- I trust I am exactly where I am supposed to be now.
- I can trust life.
- I am in harmony with divine guidance.
- I automatically live in trust.
- I trust that everything works for the highest good.

LOVE AFFIRMATIONS

- I choose love as my response to others.
- I think loving thoughts about everyone.
- I feel divine love in my heart.
- I make choices that are deeply loving.
- The love in my heart expands and grows daily.
- My intentions are always loving and kind.

- I feel deep love in my core.
- I live in an ocean of divine love.
- My love is unconditional.
- I am an expression of divine love.
- I love the divine spirit within me.

HEALING AFFIRMATIONS

- Positive healing energy flows easily through me.
- I am open to receiving divine healing.
- I surrender pain and suffering.
- I take good care of myself.
- I feel divine healing.
- My body is a holy temple.
- I am well taken care of by God.
- I receive the healing presence of God.

ABUNDANCE AFFIRMATIONS

- I am open to receive abundant gifts from God.
- I am open to all possibilities for abundance.
- I accept the abundance the universe gives me.
- I am open to receive something wonderful today.
- I receive prosperity without limits.
- I feel prosperous.
- I am a source of abundance.
- God's abundance manifests through me.

GRATITUDE AFFIRMATIONS

- I thank God for what I have.

• I am a grateful person.
• I am at peace with all I have been given.
• I am thankful for my healing and health.
• I thank God for what is revealed to me.[21]

SELF-ESTEEM

Self-Esteem is the way people think about themselves, and how worthwhile they feel. Another way to look at it is whether someone likes themselves. Someone with low self-esteem may think they are worthless or bad at things. When you have healthy self-esteem, you feel good about yourself and see yourself as deserving the respect of others. People who have high self-esteem, generally are prideful. This could be someone who has a "me, me, me" attitude or may have a sense of entitlement which can become dangerously close to narcissism.

> For by the grace [of God] given to me I say to every one of you not to think more highly of himself [and of his importance and ability] than he ought to think; but to think so as to have sound judgment, as God has apportioned to each a degree of faith [and a purpose designed for service].
>
> Romans 12:3, AMP

> But He gives us more and more grace [through the power of the Holy Spirit to defy sin and live an obedient life that reflects both our faith and our gratitude

for our salvation]. Therefore, it says, "GOD IS OP-POSED TO THE PROUD *and* HAUGHTY, BUT [continually] GIVES [the gift of] GRACE TO THE HUMBLE [who turn away from self-righteousness].

James 4:6, AMP

SIGNS OF LOW SELF-ESTEEM
- Sensitivity to criticism
- Social withdrawal
- Irritation or hostility
- Too much focus on personal problems
- Physical symptoms (fatigue, insomnia, and headaches)
- Negative thoughts about the self
- Feelings of worthlessness and defeat
- Experiencing shame after failure[22]

I struggled with low self-esteem growing up. I didn't have many things to be proud of. Most individuals base their self-esteem on their accomplishments, status, finances, or appearance. My parents struggled on a daily basis just to survive. My mother was a hard worker and she did everything she could to provide for our family and give us children nice clothing to wear to school. I struggled with appearance and self-worth. I constantly battled with my self-image. I thought I didn't have a lot to offer so I developed "self-validation" complex. I craved being noticed by others and worried what others thought of me.

When I would have really bad days, I wanted others to know my hurts, more specifically my closer friends in my circle that I trusted. I needed the constant reassurance and validation from others that I was making the right choices. I would try to justify my bad behavior. The more I would focus on it my mental state would amplify, the intense feelings would fester more rapidly, and would become overwhelming at times.

Here are some things that helped me break bad habits once and for all:

1. Tell yourself that you matter, and you are worthy. Avoid all negative self-talk.
2. Prove to yourself that you matter, and that you can overcome your insecurities.
3. Build your self-confidence with love and self-respect.
4. Forgive yourself and other people around you that caused unwanted pain.
5. Don't compare yourself to other people.
6. Learn to be more assertive.
7. Go to therapy to get the tools you need.

It's important to set yourself free from glutton punishment. It's not an easy task to overcome. It has taken me many years to recognize the agony I was putting on myself. The more you ignore the changes you need to make in life, the harder it will be to enjoy life and the people around you that you love. Please don't take life for granted. Do something about it by making the effort to break the chains that have empowered you for many years of your life.

But forget all that—it is nothing compared to what I am going to do. For I am about to do something new. See, I have already begun! Do you not see it? I will make a pathway through the wilderness. I will create rivers in the dry wasteland.

Isaiah 43:18-19, NLT

SELF-WORTH

Self-worth is at the basis of our very selves. Our thoughts, feelings, and behaviors are intimately tied into how we view our worthiness and values as a human being.

We need to start seeing ourselves through God's eyes. We all grew up with distorted images of ourselves from everybody around us. Everybody has scars and wounds. Our antidote is the truth of how God sees us. God sees us very differently than we see ourselves. With God's grace and love He sent His son Jesus to sacrifice His life so we can find the true meaning of life.

Because of his grace he made us right in his sight and gave us confidence that we will inherit eternal life.

Titus 3:7, NLT

Perspective is looking through, seeing clearly; the capacity to view things in their true relation of relative importance. Allow yourself to see God's way of seeing. When your self-worth is being jeopardized speak God's truth over yourself.

1. Never picture yourself in any other circumstance or place.
2. Never compare yourself to others when others may have more than you.
3. Never allow yourself to complain about anything, but be humble with what you have.
4. Never allow yourself to dwell on tomorrow. Remember that tomorrow is a new day-it's God's worry, not yours.
5. Never allow yourself to wish for more than what God has already promised for your life. Be thankful for what He has given you. There is meaning to everything that God has planned for your life.

CONTENT WHATEVER THE CIRCUMSTANCES

I'm glad in God, far happier than you would ever guess—happy that you're again showing such strong concern for me. Not that you ever quit praying and thinking about me. You just had no chance to show it. Actually, I don't have a sense of needing anything personally. I've learned by now to be quite content whatever my circumstances. I'm just as happy with little as with much, with much as with little. I've found the recipe for being happy whether full or hungry, hands full or hands empty. Whatever I have, wherever I am, I can make it through anything in the One who makes me who I am. I don't mean that your help didn't mean a lot to me—it did. It was a beautiful thing that you came alongside me in my troubles.

Philippians 4:11-14, MSG

There will be difficult days. Discover some things about yourself that are true in the eyes of God. Let God set you free from the bondage of anxiety, hardships, distractions, and feelings of self- control. Let God use your story for a purpose by letting Him be the vessel in your life. Let God be your representations of your old life to share your life story of pain, disappointments, failures, worthless emotions about yourself, self-pity, hatred, envy, control and distortion of the way you see yourself. Let's agree to release those pains that we have struggled with for so long that have held us back in life.

Our lives are valuable in the eyes of God. We must seek the reflection of God and not let anyone have the power in your life to make you feel anything that is not true. Let's agree to break free from the lies that you allowed the enemy to tell you.

I want to share a story from 2005 where God used me for good. I met a sweet young teen that came through my path in my walk of healing on my journey. God used my life as an instrument to speak Truth to her. We had similar backgrounds from being molested, and she had a difficult time breaking free of the pain and the demons that were inside of her and holding her back. That day I shared my life story with her. I knew God was speaking through me to her.

God designed us both to work in His glory in a powerful and spiritual way. I had a vision that God was going to use our stories for good to help reach millions of people from the same hurts we experienced. The Holy Spirit was speaking through me so heavily to her. The vision was so clear to me. His message was spoken through me to her as a faithful servant. God wanted me to share the truth with her that she needed to humbly wait for Him; that He had a plan for her future. He was speaking His words through me to enlighten her heart by renewing her life and starting a new beginning by being set free from the bondage that was keeping her tied down to the floor so tight. She needed to let God cut the rope loose and allow Him to carry her out of the darkness to allow herself to be seen in God's righteousness. His path was being laid out before her.

God's glory and honor for her was to heal her, teach her a new life to walk by molding her to be released of her faults, weaknesses, desires of self-destruction, and her family curse. God wanted her to see herself as His beautiful bride, and He was going to use her as a strong Christian leader, amazing friend, incredible wife and mentor for other young girls out there. He saw how magnificent she was, and He wanted her to see that about herself too. Through Christ alone He would give her strength of His glory and power to protect her and make the necessary changes to her mind to see herself like rubies. He wanted her to see no more inflictions but peace that affirmed who God said she was. She was not flawed but beautiful, valued, and beloved by God. She was no longer a wilted flower, but a flower that bloomed so radiant.

We must face ourselves in the mirror and not be ashamed of what we see in our own reflection. The reflection that we see is a secure chosen servant of God who has a higher calling and will no longer have a permanent black mark in our souls.

I am Beautiful:

You are altogether beautiful, my darling, beautiful in every way.

Song of Solomon 4:7, NLT

She is clothed with strength and dignity, and she laughs without fear of the future.

Proverbs 31:25, NLT

The Lord will hold you in his hand for all to see—a splendid crown in the hand of God.

Isaiah 62:3, NLT

My beloved spoke and said to me, "Arise, my darling, my beautiful one, come with me."

Song of Solomon 2:10, NIV

She opens her mouth with wisdom, and the teaching of kindness is on her tongue.

Proverbs 31:26, ESV

I AM VALUABLE:

> Blessed is she who has believed that the Lord would fulfill his promises to her!
>
> Luke 1:45, NIV
>
> God is within her; she will not fall; God will help her a break of day.
>
> Psalm 46:5, NIV

> You were bought at a price. Therefore honor God with your bodies.
>
> 1 Corinthians 6:20, NIV

> She is worth far more than rubies.
>
> Proverbs 31:10, NIV

> I have been crucified with Christ and I no longer live, but Christ lives in me. The life I now live in the body, I live by faith in the Son of God, who loved me and gave himself for me.
>
> Galatians 2:20, NIV

Christ alone will strengthen us with His glory and power to protect us. He will change our minds to think like He thinks so He can work in our lives. To finish the story about my sweet friend, she is now married to an incredible Christian man. They both serve at their church. She is an inspirational/transformation speaker, coach and leadership trainer with The John

Maxwell Team. She is a writer and has her own business that helps with character training. She has also done Pastoral Care at Life Church. God is good all the time. Once we are able to get over our fears, God has unlimited resources for our lives. He will do amazing work in us.

SELF-BELIEF

Have confidence in your own abilities or judgment. This is an important quality to have, as without the ability to believe in your own worth and actions you may struggle to reach your full potential and live a less fulfilling life.

When people don't believe in their decision-making, they can become indecisive and less willing to take risks. If you struggle with believing in your abilities or being intelligent enough, this can cause doubt within yourself affect your confidence to make a sound decision because of the lack of belief in yourself.

One of the biggest reasons I fell in love with my husband was because of his strength in believing in himself. He is a strong man with high confidence in himself. He is a leader among leaders and brings strength to our family. When obstacles stand in our path, he never falters with fear but instead he rises up to the occasion and takes authority, making the sound and swift decisions to better our family to move forward. He is a truly unique and one of a kind Man of God.

My husband has a brave heart and fights for change on the Reservation where he works. He is the Chief of Police & Supervisory Special Agent trying to make a positive difference in other Native American lives that many don't have the opportunity to have. He makes it his mission to help them to develop a positive mindset, encouraging them to believe in themselves and to embrace the spirit of their ancestors. He has the utmost belief in his abilities and that he will achieve his aspirations by making a clear path to bring perspective into their lives and works diligently to help them to believe in change.

He wants to help break the substance abuse in the community and encourage them to overcome addiction and self-destructive behaviors to better their tribe. So many tribes have the same things in common when it comes to despair on our sovereign reservations. After so many generations of displacement at the hands of our government it has caused widespread poverty, neglect, and entrapment in the endless cycle of never-ending hopelessness that leads to violent crimes more than "three times higher than the national average on our reservations."[23]

In the reservation communities there is an overwhelming risk for suicide, murder, and assault. My husband wants to help his people break the curse of dysfunctional behavior and take pride in their cultural heritage as so many of them try to do on a daily basis. So many people don't understand what is going on in their world and never will. We are blissfully ignorant to their cultural problems since our own government forced them off their land over and over throughout history. Most people don't realize the serious poverty they face through having some of the most geographically isolated locations. This makes for some of the poorest educational and nutritional opportunities, along with housing, that rivals any third-world country's living. Most Native Americans don't know anything different and have what many call a "reservation mindset". They are so used to this lifestyle that they don't understand how unhealthy it really is for the children living in these environments, and feel as if they cannot escape it or do better.

To give some perspective on what he has to see on a daily basis may cause many to doubt or not even comprehend. My husband was working with his Patrol Officers when he got a call for an assault of a thirteen-year-old. He was the first person on the scene, and he worked to save her life for twenty minutes until the ambulance arrived. Not only was he the first person to respond wearing his Police hat, but he then put his Special Agent hat on and spent more than a week investigating and chasing down leads with the FBI. He then made the arrest of the nineteen-year-old who committed this terrible crime.

He had a hard time with this girl being close to our daughter's age, and he struggled emotionally. This struck him to the core of his heart and soul. No matter how it impacted him, he was determined to find the person that assaulted this child. This child of God was in such terrible condition, near death, but God was victorious and gave my husband the strength and determination to find this person and seek justice for her. This poor sweet girl was the victim of a tragic event and her innocence was stolen from her in such a tragic way. All the pain she has endured will cause great mistrust in others throughout the rest of her life. This breaks my heart and is even more the reason why I want to help innocent children that have been victimized by incomprehensible violence.

> Yes, my soul, find rest in God; my hope comes from him. Truly he is my rock and my salvation; he is my fortress; I will not be shaken.
>
> Psalm 62:5-6, NIV

SELF-CONFIDENCE

The self-assurance in one's personal judgment that increases from experiences of having mastered particular activities. It is a positive belief that in the future one can generally accomplish what one wishes to do.

Your level of self-confidence can show in many ways: your behavior, your body language, how you speak, what you say, and so on. Look at the following comparisons of common confident behavior with behavior associated with low self-confidence. Which thoughts or actions do you recognize in yourself and people around you?

CONFIDENT BEHAVIOR	BEHAVIOR ASSOCIATED WITH LOW SELF-CONFIDENCE
Doing what you believe to be right, even if others mock or criticize you for it.	Governing your behavior based on what other people think.
Being willing to take risks and go the extra mile to achieve better things.	Staying in your comfort zone, fearing failure, and so avoid taking risks.
Admitting your mistakes and learning from them.	Working hard to cover up mistakes and hoping that you can fix the problem before anyone notices.
Waiting for others to congratulate you on your accomplishments.	Extolling your own virtues as often as possible to as many people as possible.
Accepting compliments graciously. "Thanks, I really worked hard on that prospectus. I'm pleased you recognize my efforts."	Dismissing compliments offhandedly. "Oh, that prospectus was nothing really, anyone could have done it."

As you can see from these examples, low self-confidence can be self-destructive, and it often manifests itself as negativity. Confident people are generally more positive – they believe in themselves and their abilities, and they also believe in living life to the full.[24]

I saw this chart and wanted to share with you. I thought this could be handy for you to see the difference between confidence and low self-confidence. If you would like to read more about it, visit the website.

GOD HEALS AND RESTORES THE LOST

I would like to share a journey of my mother's that was inspirational in her walk with God, bringing healing and restoration to their relationship so that she found her way back to God.

On July 5, 2015 my mother and my stepdad decided to take the motorcycle for a drive around the lake. They were enjoying the nice weather that day, spending time together and letting the wind blow in their face. This day seemed like any other day they had together but this time it was different. A car ran a red light and struck my parents. The driver wasn't paying attention-he was texting and driving-when all of the sudden my parents rode through the green light on their side.

The driver hit them both and they flew off the motorcycle. My stepdad was trying to protect my mother, so he turned his motorcycle to avoid the immediate contact on my mother's side. When the car and motorcycle collided together, they both were hurt really bad. My stepdad hit his head hard on the cement and it caused immediate brain damage and broke his leg. My mother had a broken pelvis and several rib fractures along with some eternal bleeding that had to be stopped.

They were rushed to the hospital by ambulance. My stepdad was not able to be saved. They tried to search for brain activity for several hours but there was none to be found. He was being kept on life support with a breathing machine to keep him alive. The family had to come together to agree to take him off the life support. My mother was out of it and they rolled her bed next to his so she could tell him goodbye. That moment was so heartbreaking. My mother tried to crawl out of bed just to touch his hand and kiss him and hold him tight. She was screaming and crying for him not to be taken away and not to leave her.

While all of this was going on, I was rushing to see my parents in the hospital, trying to make it before the doctors took him off life support, but I didn't make it. It took me over four hours to get there. I didn't get to say goodbye to him, but I was able to be there for the family and spend time with them during the aftermath of this terrible accident.

My mother was in the hospital for about a month before being released. She couldn't go to her husband's funeral because of how bad of shape she was in physically. When she was released, she was in a wheelchair for three months and couldn't take care of herself. I moved her in with me so I could help my mother get better and recover from her wounds, but mentally her wounds were not yet healed.

She walked around with a walker and cane for about six months before she could walk completely without anything supporting her. She was depressed for a long time after losing the love of her life. Her self-confidence was destroyed. She had let her husband be the leader in the family. He took in my mother, my two younger siblings, and my cousins when my mother got divorced from my birth father. She finally found someone she loved deeply and trusted.

He was a kind and gentle man to my mother. He brought her out of a deep hole of despair when my parents got divorced. She had never met a man that truly loved all of her and didn't want anything in return, just my mother's love. He wanted to be a provider for the family. He took care of everything: the bills, house, banking, vehicles, etc. They were so wonderful together. It was amazing to see my mother so happy after being in an unhealthy marriage for over twenty years with my birth father. After my stepfather's death, my mother was lost without him. She was overwhelmed and felt defeated. She had to learn to take baby steps to be more independent.

God showed His love through me. I hated to see my mother go through all the pain she was experiencing. I encouraged her to get out of the house so she wouldn't stay in her room and get depressed, or isolate herself from everyone. Little by little she started to gain confidence. She started to go to church with us as a family. She went to a women's Bible study with me and she started to go to a Christian counselor to get her wounds off her chest from the devastating loss. I started to see the light come back into her face. She wanted to start taking care of herself and was having fun getting dressed up. We started to go shopping together. It was a bonding moment between my mother and me. It was something we did together when I was younger that I treasured. It was one of the happier moments we had together when we were off at the mall just being girls without any worries in the world. We lived in the moment.

She started to do therapy to build her muscle strength back up, then she went to the gym with me too, to help her body heal faster. We took her to get her hair colored and cut, got her nails done, and took her to a Gala event that my husband had. She was finally seeing the light at the end of the tunnel. Her hope was being restored and she started to believe in herself again that she could make it on her own. Through God's love and grace, He gave her the necessary tools she needed to overcome the struggles of dependency and find her way back to Jesus' hands.

We built a new relationship together between mother and daughter that I will cherish for the rest of my life. God not only healed my mother's wounds, but also healed mine that had been broken at a young age in my life. We became really close and found a new common ground of faith with God together that we needed. I forgave my mother and was able to open up and have a better relationship with her. This is what we needed from each other. I am so blessed that God restored the brokenness and the bond that once was shattered. God mended us back together and I am so thankful for what God can has done for our family to grow closer together.

Through all the trials that my mother had to face, she always pressed through the tough times, even when she felt defeated and wanted to give up. She was holding on by a thread, but she didn't let her life hold her hostage by pain. She got back up, brushed the grass off her knees, nursed her wounds back to health, and started to press back hard and let God fight her battles for her. She was more than determined to fight for her children and she said, "enough is enough" with the abuse. She broke off the chains that were restricting her.

There is beauty in what God has done for my mom. Being her daughter, watching her go through trial after trial, I was given hope to overcome my own journey by seeing through that my mother didn't give up even when she was at her lowest point. I would think of what my mother went through, and how she was a survivor. If she could do it so could I.

I believe I got the best of my mother being a warrior. She is a hardworking woman and she learned to not let life problems defeat her. She picked up the sword and started to swing back at the enemy. God is so good. My mother was able to go back to work, buy a home in her name all by herself for the first time, and has been there for my two younger siblings. She has never been so close to the family.

She is no longer an introvert, and she was able to mend her relationship with her mother, sister, and brother as well. She was able to be there for my grandma and uncle up to their last days here on earth before they passed away. She finally started to put herself back out there by being vulnerable. She started to get out of her house more and more to grow a new bond with all of her family. This woman has learned to be a self-confident person. I am honored to call her my mother. She is a true overcomer.

"The Lord is building up Jerusalem; He is gathering [together] the exiles of Israel. He heals the brokenhearted And binds up their wounds [healing their pain and comforting their sorrow]. He counts the number of the stars; He calls them all by their names.

Great is our [majestic and mighty] Lord and abundant in strength; His understanding is inexhaustible [infinite, boundless]. The Lord lifts up the humble; He casts the wicked down to the ground.

Psalm 147:2-6, AMP

SELF-LOVE

Self-love is having a high regard for your own well-being and happiness. It means taking care of your own needs and not sacrificing your well-being to please others. You are not settling for less than you deserve.

This is someone who is comfortable in their own skin, confident, and accepts all of their self through the bad and ugly. They take care of their personal needs, wants, desires, and health. They are not deterred from someone's outside opinion, but press through their goals, passions, happiness, dreams, and desires.

I learned throughout my life if I cannot love myself first, then I don't have the capability to love another human being until I am right with myself. I realized after being out of dysfunctional relationships that I could see why I was choosing these guys to begin with. I was living a destructive life and living a careless lifestyle because I didn't love or respect myself.

Once I started to truly love myself is when I was able to stop the bad behavior. I did this to myself for many years. I learned to have a more fulfilling life once I was able to recognize what I was doing. What I found was that looking pretty, having nice clothes, having nice cars and home, and having money wasn't going to buy me happiness more love for myself. I was only deceiving myself with luxury of satisfaction providing a gratifying, short-term good feeling, but that soon would dissipate.

We must learn to appreciate ourselves first in order to grow, and take actions to move forward with support of our psychological mindset and spiritual growth. We must take the responsibility to learn from our actions and allow them to mature us. For many years I wanted to find meaning in my life and I struggled with self-doubt in overcoming my life purpose and values. I needed to take full ownership of my mistakes, short-comings, and weaknesses so I could expand my mind. Things that I did that may help you:

1. Become mindful of your thoughts, feelings, and wants rather than worrying what others want from you.

2. Act on what you *need* rather than what you *want*. There are things in life you must turn away from that may give you a temporary feeling of excitement or good feeling in the heat of the moment. We need to stay strong and center ourselves to move forward in life. Break the patterns that trouble you and keep you stuck in the past.

3. Practice good self-care. We must take care of our basic needs such as daily healthy activity, eating better, exercising, getting the proper amount of sleep, and having healthy social interactions. Pray more and worry less.

4. Set boundaries and set limits to learn to say no to things that suck the life out of you and cause harm or deplete you physically, emotionally, and spiritually. Don't let a person define you.

5. Protect yourself. We must attract the right kind of people in our lives. There are some people in your life that will take pleasure in your pain, rather than your happiness and success. There is not enough time in life to spend wasting any on people feeding off of your weaknesses.

6. Forgive yourself. Stop being so hard on yourself. Stop punishing yourself with all the mistakes you have made but learn from them so you can grow. Accept all of your imperfections. Practice being less hard on yourself. There are no failures in life when you learn and grown from them; there are only lessons to learn.

7. Live intentionally. You will learn to love yourself more when you work for your purpose in life that God designed you for. Set goals that are healthy, and this will bring you purpose in life and the tools you need to overcome your struggles that once defined you.

Love is the very mechanism of growth in your life. For the parents out there, think of a time in your child's life where they were learning to take their first steps to walk. They would walk a little then fall, then they picked themselves back up with your encouragement helping them to get back on their feet and hold themselves up. They tried and tried again until they succeeded.

They didn't know anything differently. The nature of a child is to continue trying and learning to develop.

Every infant naturally feels love and happiness. The child is dependent on us to feel safe and to be taken care of. We, as parents, praise them for their efforts and give them confidence throughout their adventure in life. We encourage them to embrace their emotions. We teach them morals; to be compassionate and kind; to love; to encourage others; and teach them the core of their spiritual relationship with Christ.

The paradox is to have realization that God wants more of us. He wants us to truly love ourselves. He wants us to put energy into things that are important. God gives us encouragement to have the determination to seek His love and let Him guide our paths. He wants to walk right next to us and hold our hands throughout the process. He wants to appear in your walk and adventure alongside you. The ultimate love that God has given us was His son Jesus to die for our sins. True love is courageous by God's creation that is good, and your life has a greater plan, for which we are responsible for.

If our hearts condemn us, we know that God is greater than our hearts, and he knows everything.

1 John 3:20, NIV

9

I am Rescued, Redeemed, Restored, and Forgiven

You have rescued us from dark powers and brought us safely into the kingdom of Your Son, whom You love and in whom we are redeemed and forgiven of our sins [through His blood].

Colossians 1:13-14, VOICE

PARABLE OF THE GOOD SAMARITAN
Jesus replied, "A man was going down from Jerusalem to Jericho, and he encountered robbers, who stripped him of his clothes [and belongings], beat him, and went their way [unconcerned], leaving him half dead. Now by coincidence a priest was going down that road, and when he saw him, he passed by on the other side. Likewise a Levite also came down to the place and saw him, and passed by on the other side [of the road]. But a Samaritan (foreigner), who was travel-

ing, came upon him; and when he saw him, he was deeply moved with compassion [for him], and went to him and bandaged up his wounds, pouring oil and wine on them [to sooth and disinfect the injuries]; and he put him on his own pack-animal, and brought him to an inn and took care of him. On the next day he took out two denarii (two days' wages) and gave them to the innkeeper, and said, 'Take care of him; and whatever more you spend, I will repay you when I return.' Which of these three do you think proved himself a neighbor to the man who encountered the robbers?" He answered, "The one who showed compassion and mercy to him." Then Jesus said to him, "Go and constantly do the same.

Luke 10:30-37, AMP

RESCUED

I would like to share a little more about my father's journey. In some of my earlier chapters I spoke about his alcohol addiction and being in and out of jail for multiple DUI's. Once he was finally released from jail for the last time in his life he met a wonderful woman he eventually married. He was doing wonderfully then slowly he started to drink again until it was once again consuming his life. However, this time his wife reached out to me to say that my father wasn't doing well.

My father was hallucinating, and something was off about him. My father is in construction and does cement work. She expressed her concern with me that there was something wrong. He thought he was at work pouring cement at a job site but really he was in his home on the bathroom floor doing the movements as if he was pouring cement and smoothing it out. He also thought the glass he was drinking out of had wheels on it, and that his wife was sleeping with a caveman from the Geico commercial. I know these details may seem funny, but there was definitely something wrong with him.

At the time I wasn't married yet, but I was dating my husband when I got the phone call. I was driving in the car with my (now) husband and we had to rush over there to try to convince him to go to the hospital because he kept refusing. Keep in mind that my husband hadn't yet met my father and we were in the early stages of dating. I was embarrassed for him to see my father that way for the first time meeting him, but my husband was so loving and kind and reassured me everything would be okay. He wanted to be there for me and to help my father.

He is incredible with his words. He was soft-spoken to my father and talked to him like he had known him forever. He finally helped convince my father to get in the car with us to take a drive and as we drove he headed toward the hospital. When we pulled up my father refused to go in. So my husband asked him to come in because his buddy from the military was at the hospital and wasn't doing well so he wanted to check on him. After about thirty minutes my father finally agreed. Once we got in the doors, we persuaded him, "Since we are here why don't you just see a doctor to check you out?" It was important to us to get my father in the hospital because no one could reason with him. He wasn't being himself and something was wrong with his decision-making.

Eventually he was able to be seen in the ER and they put him in a room to be checked out and do blood work. The doctor ran multiple tests on him. They found that his potassium levels were so low that it was causing his psychosis to be off, causing him to be delirious and hallucinate. It was so bad that it almost led to his death but by the grace of God we got him seen right away. This was happening to my father because he was on weeks of excess alcohol consumption. His electrolyte disturbance was causing his magnesium and calcium to be low as well.

The doctor was able to get my father in better shape and got his potassium levels back up. He stayed in the hospital for a couple days for observation. This event was eye opening for my dad. He realized that he didn't want to go back down that same rabbit hole of drinking excessively like he did before when he was with my mother. He wanted something better for him and his wife. He decided from that day forward to live a much better life.

He has now been married to his wife for over fourteen years. He is happier now with his new life. He has chosen to overcome what was taking control over his life. He has been able to maintain freedom from his addiction by overcoming his lifestyle of repeat bad behavior and alcohol abuse. He has been a great dad to my stepmom's kids. He is a proud papa. His health isn't the greatest from all the damage he did to his body over the years. It led him to have cirrhosis of the liver from too much alcohol consumption for so many years; COPD; and emphysema to his lungs from excess smoking.

He stays home the majority of the time and helps babysit or take his step-grandkids to school. He still does some concrete work but it's not so easy for his body anymore. I learned to forgive my dad and see the real reason why he struggled throughout his life. He had a hard life when he was a kid as well. It has been a vicious cycle of never-ending alcohol abuse and neglect. He learned this behavior from his parents, and it has been throughout the family history.

I decided that I wanted to stop this cycle with me and try to not repeat the same behavior to my children so they could be better than me, and give their children a better representation of what true love looks like when God is the center of the family that holds the family strong and knitted together. God has rescued my father from suicide, prevented him from killing someone else from drinking and driving, gave him a new start in a healthy marriage, ended the abuse cycle, gave him happiness with his family again, brought healing to his spirit, and most importantly my father got saved when he was in jail. God gave him a new leaf to turn.

> O Lord, I have come to you for protection; don't let me be disgraced. Save me, for you do what is right. Turn your ear to listen to me; rescue me quickly. Be my rock of protection, a fortress where I will be safe. You are my rock and my fortress. For the honor of your name, lead me out of this danger. Pull me from the

trap my enemies set for me, for I find protection in you alone. I entrust my spirit into your hand. Rescue me, Lord, for you are a faithful God. I hate those who worship worthless idols. I trust in the Lord. I will be glad and rejoice in your unfailing love, for you have seen my troubles, and you care about the anguish of my soul. You have not handed me over to my enemies but have set me in a safe place.

Psalm 31:1-8, NLT

We must trust God that He will rescue us through any circumstances we are in. There will be times throughout our lives that we will walk in darkness and be shaken to our core; where we cannot see light in the middle of the situation we are in. We may not see what God is doing behind the scenes, but He is preparing His way in our souls to heal us beyond what we could ever imagine. God has a marvelous plan and we need to have a clear vision and open ears to listen to what our precious God is trying to show us through our pain and hurt. There has to be preparation to reconstruct change in us. God has to work out the imperfections in our souls in order to be used for God's glory here on earth. Look what Jesus had to do for our uncleanliness so we could be made whole with Him:

Yet it was our weaknesses he carried; it was our sorrows[a] that weighed him down. And we thought his troubles were a punishment from God, a punishment for his own sins! But he was pierced for our rebellion, crushed for our sins. He was beaten so we could be whole. He was whipped so we could be healed. All of us, like sheep, have strayed away. We have left God's paths to follow our own. Yet the Lord laid on him the sins of us all.

Isaiah 53:4-6, NLT

As a result, an amazing change has been taking place in our relationship with God. Through His son, Jesus, we may now enter into the Holy of Holies in heaven with Him when our time has come to go home. Nothing is impossible for our God in any circumstance we are in. He has already won the battle for us.

REDEEMED

My precious Father has redeemed my soul. Through the heartbreaks and tears, God brought abundant joy in my life. When I finally learned to redirect my bad habits with good ones that is when God changed my heart for good to make wise decisions. Ask yourself a question, "What areas in your life do you need to recognize that you need to change, so God can redeem your soul?" What are you unwilling to give up that is causing the most hindrance with your walk with God? Is it unhealthy relationships, sex before marriage, partying, talking down to yourself, co-dependencies, lying, reckless behavior, lust, envy, anger, etc.? We must learn to overcome life obstacles, but still enjoy living. God has taught me to break through all that mess that was holding me back to allow the book of my life journey to unfold for others to see through all my vulnerabilities, mistakes, shame, pride, and fears.

> Finally, believers, whatever is true, whatever is honorable *and* worthy of respect, whatever is right *and* confirmed by God's word, whatever is pure *and* wholesome, whatever is lovely *and* brings peace, whatever is admirable and of good repute; if there is any excellence, if there is anything worthy of praise, think *continually* on these things [center your mind on them, and implant them in your heart].
>
> Philippians 4:8, AMP

As believers here on earth God will watch how we handle our challenges in life. It's not the challenges that come in our paths that can bring your spirit down. It's how we respond to those situations when we are faced with them.

1. Learn to create your own reality. Picture in your mind what you want, by seeing your future, past, and current self. Pay attention to where your thoughts go.
2. See yourself worthy and speak life-giving words to your soul.
3. See things through God's eyes, not by man. He sees your beauty, strength, bravery, persistence, and empowerment to change for the better.

God knows it's a process and it's not simple. It requires a new way of thinking, acting, and having greater ambition to make new effort to engage in a whole life change. We must acknowledge God in everything. God deserves first place before anything else. We need to seek God's purpose in our life pain. Our flesh in us wants its way. We must submit our flesh to God. Our flesh can be strong and convincing to seek worldly desires. If we want change in our lives, we have to expect something from God, and have faith that God will deliver. Be a person of faith.

We got pregnant again two months after our sweet little girl was born on Feb 7, 2008. On June 6, 2008, I went to the hospital to do a normal checkup and exam on the growth of our second baby. I was only eight weeks pregnant. My husband took off to come meet me at the hospital on the military base. He was active duty in the Army during this time in NC. The nurse took my husband and I back in a room to do our ultrasound. When they were moving around on my belly to find the baby's heartbeat for us to hear, they couldn't find the heartbeat. The nurse had a concerned look, then got the doctor to confirm what she thought may have happened to the baby.

The doctor explained to us as comforting as possible, that our baby's heartbeat stopped and the baby hadn't grown but had passed away. When the news was told to us I went numb from shock and an overwhelming surge of anxiety and panic hit me. My face filled up with heat and I looked at my husband and started to cry. My husband held me, and we started to cry together. The doctor left our room to give us a moment to collect our emotions.

God blessed me with an incredible husband who was so supportive and compassionate to me after the horrific news we had just received. I broke down, devastated to find out that they had to do an emergency dilation and curettage, a surgical procedure they perform in or after the first trimester of a woman who has a miscarriage. We were both in shock that the doctor was going to have to perform this on me right then and there when we had come in just to have a simple checkup.

It became one of my biggest nightmares having lost a child. I was distraught. The doctor sedated me during the procedure and when I woke up I was crying hysterically. I had an immediate feeling of emptiness inside me and knew my baby was gone. It was bad enough my body was going through so many hormonal changes, and this made it ten times worse. I couldn't stop crying for hours. My poor husband had to go back to work after hearing this terrible news, to deal with a situation with another military soldier. I felt like something got ripped out of me and was stolen.

It took a long time of healing before I could get past what happened to my husband and me. Being young newlyweds and parents to another little girl was a trying stage in our marriage. This was a lot for us to handle in such a short time of being married. My husband and I just focused all of our energy on being the best parents to our sweet little girl. I was not a perfect mother. I had a lot of highs and lows after the loss and my body changes. I would sometimes be short with my daughter and had outbursts of anger. I didn't realize it at the time, but I was hurting so badly that I was taking out my frustrations on her and she didn't deserve that from me.

A lot of unwanted emotions came to the surface that I didn't realize I had that needed to be dealt with, such as the pain I endured as a child myself. Sometimes in life you don't realize difficult feelings you need to work on until you are a mother or father. It's a new experience that comes new feelings that you never felt before. Sometimes I would struggle with empathy toward her. I think that comes to the way I was brought up, not having the affection I needed as a child. So, this was a new emotion I needed to learn and I had to work on re-wiring my mind to be more sensitive to other people's feelings rather than my own selfish needs.

I couldn't be careless any longer. There was another innocent child depending on me to be the most loving mother to her. I was so scared to be a parent and I didn't want to make the same mistakes as my parents. But sometimes the harder I tried not to be my parents, the more I could see some things in me that were being brought up to the surface that were like my parents and that frightened me. I had to care for another human being which requires great responsibility.

I had to get things under control. I decided to get help and seek guidance from other women of God. I got involved in a lot of Bible studies, mostly Beth Moore. I looked up to a lady at my church and she led the Bible studies at her home and sometimes at the church. I felt like I could talk to her about anything. She gave me the inspiration to move on from my hurts and taught me what I needed to do to be a mother to my baby girl, and be the wife I needed to be to my husband.

In the midst of my darkest moments, God intervened in my circumstances and heard my cry. He truly redeemed my soul and allowed me to move forward in healing in my walk with Christ. God turns our curse or nightmare into a blessing. There is a reason for everything. I learned to cast all my anxieties to God and keep my faith that He would bring healing because He cares for me deeply. God taught me to find rest in my soul. I am a warrior of God.

> Calling the crowd to join his disciples, he said, "Anyone who intends to come with me has to let me lead. You're not in the driver's seat; I am. Don't run from suffering; embrace it. Follow me and I'll show you how. Self-help is no help at all. Self-sacrifice is the way, my way, to saving yourself, your true self. What good would it do to get everything you want and lose you, the real you? What could you ever trade your soul for?
>
> Mark 8:36, MSG

> Bless and affectionately praise the LORD, O my soul, And all that is [deep] within me, bless His holy name. Bless and affectionately praise the LORD, O my soul, And do not forget any of His benefits; Who forgives all your sins, Who heals all your diseases; Who redeems your life from the pit, Who crowns you [lavishly] with

lovingkindness and tender mercy; Who satisfies your years with good things, So that your youth is renewed like the [soaring] eagle.

Psalm 103:1-5, AMP

RESTORED

When you go through a long fight against the enemy that brings difficult trials into your path, make sure you rejoice with God and be thankful for the wins of the war that he fought for you to give you strength to overcome the hurdles. When the war has subsided, it is very important to rest and celebrate God's goodness and victory. Our Lord Almighty brought His glorious crown here for His people to bring justice. He is our protector and He will not let the enemy's hands bring wrath over you.

God brought our sorrow to joy and our mourning to celebration. Courage comes from the heart. Are you brave enough to face your fears? Can you imagine living a life without fear? When you give authority to God over your life, He can position you exactly where he needs you to be. Don't be afraid, dear sister or brother, to take a leap of faith for God to reveal your destiny he has in store for you.

> I give you all the credit, GOD—you got me out of that mess, you didn't let my foes gloat. GOD, my God, I yelled for help and you put me together. GOD, you pulled me out of the grave, gave me another chance at life when I was down-and-out.

Psalm 30:1-3, MSG

"You have turned my mourning into dancing for me;
You have taken off my sackcloth and clothed me with
joy, That my soul may sing praise to You and not be
silent. O LORD my God, I will give thanks to You
forever.

Psalm 30:11-12, AMP

My precious God changed me inside and out. He healed my
battle wounds and filled my cup with joy. God blessed me with
another child May 28, 2011. It took three years after the loss of
our child to have another baby. I thought for a long time we
couldn't get pregnant again losing our second child. Before we
got pregnant, I was taking Clomid and injections in my stomach to try to speed up getting pregnant. That didn't work so we
did an IUI and that failed so we gave up just to see if we could
naturally get pregnant again.

We went to church on a Sunday and our preacher was talking about someone in the room that had been hurt from losing
a child, and had been trying to get pregnant for some time. It
hit my husband and I to the core. We went to the front to pray
with our pastor after the service was over. We asked him if he
would pray over us to conceive another child. As the pastor was
praying over us, my husband and I started to cry. I felt something inside me change and the heavy spirits that was weighed
me down were lifted. I was immediately free and no longer a
slave to fear or worry.

That burden I had felt for so long was now dissipated and I felt restored. After we finished praying, our pastor said that when he prays over people who struggled with conceiving that usually it opened the flood gates of children being born, and it would be hard to cut off the baby making. We all laughed together. If I remember correctly, we got pregnant a month or so later. Praise Jesus. God is a God of miracles.

It was time for me to clear my mind. God spoke to my heart to take it easy and allow my body to rest and replenish my soul from everything my body had gone through. I was learning to enjoy being in the present instead of worrying about what happened to me in the past. I was focusing on the now and enjoying being a mother of two. There are times in our lives that require reflection of our spirit. We need to rebalance our bodies when we get off track and the enemy tries to pound our spirits down, throwing blows our way.

One thing I noticed I needed to work on was my patience. I was always in a hurry and in a rush with everything. I would grow impatient when things didn't go my way. It was hard for me to rest and sit still long enough to re-energize myself. I would drive my husband nuts because I wouldn't relax after a long day with the kids. Being the mother of two small children-one baby and one three-year-old-is hard to do. Kids at that age are always high maintenance and need you for everything. They depend on you left and right to feed, clothe, change diapers, breastfeed or give them a bottle, comfort them when they are in tears, make them laugh, teach them how to talk, walk, crawl, play with them and put them to nap and or bed.

By the end of the day I was exhausted, but it was so hard for me to slow down long enough to relax and spend quality time with my husband, shut my brain off, and clear my thoughts. I was used to going a hundred miles an hour, so it was something hard for me to do. I am a busy person, it's not my nature to relax.

One thing that helped me to slow down and forced me to relax and clear my thoughts was breastfeeding my son. I would go in a quiet, dark place in his room and rock him while he fed. It was so sweet to see this innocent child relying on me to survive. It was the purest love and bond between a mother and a child. This gave me such ultimate joy, happiness, and undeniable affirmation and connection to my baby that I never wanted the feeling to end. This is how God see us. His love is genuine. God's love is real; it's not fake, pretend, or imaginary. No one on Earth loves you more than God loves you.

> Like newborn babies [you should] long for the pure milk of the word, so that by it you may be nurtured *and* grow in respect to salvation [its ultimate fulfillment], if in fact you have [already] tasted the goodness *and* gracious kindness of the Lord.
>
> 1 Peter 2:2-3, AMP
>
> Be still and know (recognize, understand) that I am God. I will be exalted among the nations! I will be exalted in the earth.
>
> Psalm 46:10, AMP

He refreshes *and* restores my soul (life); He leads me
in the paths of righteousness for His name's sake.

Psalm 23:3, AMP

If we wish to see God restore our soul, we must take the time
to rest and replenish. If we rush from one situation to the next,
we cannot let God re-focus our minds to see His greatness in
our lives. It's also important to never giving up when times get
hard.

NEVER GIVE UP AND KEEP PRESSING FORWARD THROUGH THE PAIN

So, let's not allow ourselves to get fatigued doing
good. At the right time we will harvest a good crop if
we don't give up, or quit. Right now, therefore, every
time we get the chance, let us work for the benefit of
all, starting with the people closest to us in the community of faith.

Galatians 6:9, MSG

There have been many times in my life that I could have
thrown my hands up in the air and given in to my frustrations,
disappointments, hurdles, or failures. However, I kept pressing
forward when times got tough. I would say this is one of my
stronger qualities in my character that I got from my mother
from watching her conquer her difficult situations over and

over. She didn't completely crumble where there was no turning back.

I admire my mother for how much strength she has. She gives herself little credit. She is a strong woman but as her daughter, watching her all my life I have seen what she can do and she has pulled herself out of some bad mud pits and sink holes that could have sucked her in to die. She was able to grab a hold of God's hand to pull her out of the quicksand she was in. Don't get me wrong, there were times in my life that I got so overwhelmed that it seemed like it would be easier to quit, but my incredible husband would always encourage me to get out of the slump or pity party I was in. He reminded me to not let these things that come into my life to dictate my happiness.

You choose your happiness and what affects your soul. You must live and get through the painful moments in your life. Through all the madness that comes and goes, we must agree to live in peace during the chaos so it doesn't destroy us. Don't become the victim.

STOP IMPULSIVE DECISION-MAKING

Having impulsive behaviors, I really had to work hard to stop making hasty decisions in the heat of the moment. This came with lots of practice and prayer. I have gotten much better about this now that I am a mother and a wife. It's not all about me anymore, so whatever decision I make affects my family too. If any bad decisions were ever made there would be consequences that could affect everyone in the household.

I've tried to be careful with my words in front of the children. Sometimes when I would get upset, I wouldn't always say the kindest words. My words were like a dagger to the heart if I was pushed over the edge. This was a struggle. I had to learn to not be impulsive in my frustration and say hurtful words.

This was a bad behavior that I saw throughout my childhood with my parents. They never had anything nice to say to each other or used loving or kind words. My parents constantly yelled at each other and there were rare occasions where they spoke to each other with soft voices. Their tones were always elevated with constant hateful attitude toward one another. They would like to push each other's buttons to get the other person aggravated.

My husband really has helped me out with this. He grew up with parents who spoke to him with soft tones when he got in trouble, and explained that his behavior wasn't okay. He had structure and got grounded, had things taken away if he did something bad, had spankings when needed, and his parents would always kiss and hug him afterward. They would tell my husband they loved him so much but there were consequences to making the wrong decisions.

They tried to encourage him to do better. This was the completely opposite teaching for me. This sounded foreign and weird because I wasn't used to someone caring and wanting better for you. I know my parents loved me in their own way but they had to battle constant demons of their own and they couldn't see past the pain they were currently in. Let's go back in time with my husband and children.

Don't seek revenge or carry a grudge against any of
your people. "Love your neighbor as yourself. I am
GOD."

Lev 19:18 MSG

Also it is not good for a person to be without knowledge, And he who hurries with his feet [acting impul-
sively and proceeding without caution or analyzing
the consequences] sins (misses the mark).

Proverbs 19:2, AMP

Our family moves a lot with my husband's career. He served
in the Army and now works for the government. We have lived
in seven states in twelve years of our marriage. This is a lot of
moving and a lot of change in our family. One thing I can say
from all the moves is our family depends on each other more
since we don't have family living next to us. We learned to encourage one another, and we spend lots of family time together
which is great for our marriage and our kids.

With each state we've moved to our family has grown closer.
I know our kids love that they can always count on us and know
we will always be there for them. This has built confidence in
their character. When my husband would get a job offer in another state, we prayed a lot to make sure we were making the
right decision to move our family again. One nice thing is our
kids are still young it has not affected them much with losing
touch with their friends in school, since they have been in elementary and pre-k school.

Yes, it's exciting to move from state to state and see new places, meet new friends, and be part of many churches. Our family loves traveling together in our RV and going camping. This is a joyful time where we get to spend quality time together as a family with no interruptions from our work. We have helped many people along our path in each state we have lived in. There will be a point that our family will need to settle down, grow roots, and establish a foundation. While we are waiting for that opportunity, I asked God to use us in each new state we would move to.

There was a moment in Kansas when I knew God wanted me to be a spiritual mother to a child who was thirteen years old. She was my husband's secretary's daughter and she became our babysitter. The more time she spent with us, she grew attached and wanted to be with us all the time. She loved how my husband was caring toward her and represented what a true father is supposed to be. She watched how my husband was to our three children. She looked up to us and felt safe to be able to open up and share her feelings about what was bothering her about her father. She needed someone with an open ear to listen, who wasn't her parents. She wanted someone to mentor her, to help guide her in the right direction, along with lifting her up spiritually with Christ as she was craving. She was trying to make sense of her feelings and didn't understand how to handle all the emotions that came from the pain from the divorce and neglect from her father.

We invited her to go to church. She loved how it made her feel. She felt peace and love. The more she was around she started to call us mom and dad. She was like another daughter in our family. She grew up in similar ways that I did with a parent who abused alcohol. Her father was an alcoholic and a drug user. Her mother and father were no longer together. She had a hard time accepting that her parents weren't together any longer, and that her mother moved on and married another man that she truly adores.

This man was a wonderful husband to her kids and a good role model for them to look up to. He was a police officer and lived a meaningful life and encouraged others. He wasn't an alcoholic, didn't do any drugs, and wasn't verbally abusive to her. It was hard for her to understand that her mother and siblings were in a better environment that was safe for them all. However, in her eyes she saw a person come into their lives and steal her mother away from her dad. It took a lot of time to encourage her and help her to focus on what was more important in life which is Jesus.

I wanted her to find fulfillment in Christ instead of constantly having feelings of rejection. I saw the pain in her eyes. She reminded me of a younger me. How I desperately searched for answers and meaning for my life. She craved attention all the time and when she didn't get any affection or attention she would get upset and start acting out. When I watched her life unfold right in front of me, it hurt my soul to see her in pain. I felt God lay in my heart to be there for her and to help guide her in the right direction no matter how difficult or challenging it could be at times.

Through the four years of knowing her, she struggled, but like any normal teenager does. She grew closer to God, she started believing in herself more, building confidence that she is loved, and she started learning how to not need a boy's attention to feel satisfied. This was her biggest struggle to overcome, just like me. I believe years of experience will teach her to be strong, along with ongoing practice to not allow boys to dictate how she should feel, or take advantage of her emotions.

She struggled at times, needing that validation to feel good. She could be impulsive and make hasty decisions as a young teenager where in the past it would cause her to get in trouble at home. She would get herself into bad situations where she would lie so she wouldn't get caught. We knew when she did lie, and we would try to help her to overcome this and to not be fearful of being honest even if she was worried about the consequences. We explained to her it was much worse to lie than to confess what she did.

She may have learned the hard way, but she is doing so much better now than she was before. She has a lot of life to live and she will have good and bad moments. I want her life to not be defined by her past with her father, but to be fulfilled with God. Our Heavenly Father is the true representation what a father should be and is. I want her life not to be a victim, but an overcomer. God will provide her with everything she will ever need in life and that is His love. God gave His son up to sacrifice His life for our sins so we would not perish in hell but to live all eternity with beautiful blessings with Him.

Prayer:

Thank You, Jesus, for putting this sweet precious girl in our path and entrusting us to help encourage her to want better in life. We ask that You will always be with her and help her to see value in herself that she is worthy of unconditional love no matter how her earthly father may treat her. Help her to respect and appreciate that You have so much in store for her that she may not see. We thank You so much that You have reached out and grabbed a hold of her tightly to bring protection in her life. Thank You for shielding her and putting Your angels to fight for her innocence all around her and fighting the war for her so she can see the true meaning of pure love. In Jesus Name Amen.

With what shall I come before the Lord [to honor Him] And bow myself before God on high? Shall I come before Him with burnt offerings, With yearling calves? Will the Lord be delighted with thousands of rams, Or with ten thousand rivers of oil? Shall I present my firstborn for my acts of rebellion, The fruit of my body for the sin of my soul? He has told you, O man, what is good; And what does the Lord require of you Except to be just, and to love [and to diligently practice] kindness (compassion), And to walk hubly with your God [setting aside any overblown sense of importance or self-righteousness]?

Micah 6:6-8, AMP

FORGIVEN

> Jesus prayed, "Father, forgive them; they don't know
> what they're doing." Dividing up his clothes, they
> threw dice for them. The people stood there star-
> ing at Jesus, and the ringleaders made faces, taunt-
> ing, "He saved others. Let's see him save himself! The
> Messiah of God—ha! The Chosen—ha!"
>
> Luke 23:34-35, MSG

Forgiveness is one of the hardest things you can do with your healing process. If we allow that built up anger to take control of us it can bring bitterness to our hearts. This can cause destructive behavior to act out from what is bringing hatred or underlying issues into your heart. It can cause it to become hard and numb.

For many years of my life this one thing was hard for me to do. I really had to give all my pain to God for me to find forgiveness in my heart and soul to my perpetrators who took away my innocence. I had to learn to get rid of extra baggage that was weighing me down and was clouding my judgment. I used to hit one stumbling block after another that brought me back down to my victim mindset. I had to learn to be able to recognize and identify the traits to renew my mind and follow Biblical principles. This is what victim mentality looks like.

What Is a Victim Mentality? For example, someone with a victim mentality can feel pleasure when she receives attention or pity as a result of her misfortune. She may also get a perverse "thrill" from showing off the injury caused by others and creating a sense of guilt.[25]

We must stop feeling like a victim once and for all and learn to forgive.

1. Stop blaming others for your pain. This can make you feel powerless and hopeless. We must take responsibility for our own actions when we make poor decisions.

2. We need to learn compassion toward ourselves. We must stop the behavior of self-hatred toward others and ourselves, and break the habit of self-loathing or punishing ourselves for the mistakes we have done or have been done to us.

3. Learn to be grateful and have a gratitude. This is a daily practice we must use to help us to overcome our circumstances. Be thankful for the lessons you have learned through the difficult times so you can teach others how to overcome their own pain.

4. We must learn how to resist self-sabotage. If we don't understand the true nature of happiness and it is not a natural feeling to have, we can tend to jeopardize our feelings and turn around and sabotage ourselves from experiencing joy to reverting to the pain and suffering.

5. Perform acts of kindness toward others. When we focus on doing something nice for others, we tend to

stop dwelling on our own thoughts that can keep us hostage from the freedom of happiness.

6. We must learn to forgive and let go. Victims often hold on to the feeling of bitterness and resentment of others along with anger for their past hurts.

7. Build self-confidence in yourself. People who have a victim mindset struggle with this because they normally have low self-esteem.

8. Find the source of your learned helplessness behavior. When we have a chronic longer-term victim, mentality is typically learned from childhood or early adulthood experience.

9. Shift your mentality from that of a victim, to a survivor or overcomer.

10. Challenge yourself every day to become a warrior who can fight to overcome any obstacles that come your way.[26]

I paraphrased these words on some of the things that I read at this website. You may find it interesting to look it up to read more.

As you go through life and make mistakes along your journey, admit when you are wrong and forgive yourself so you can enjoy life the way God intended for you to. There will be peaks and valleys through your journey walking with the Lord. Give yourself credit that you can do great things, and your life does have a purpose and meaning. If we have unresolved issues or resentment in our hearts it can destroy us. It's like the enemy attacking you at night when you are most vulnerable and least expecting the hit. We must always be on guard and keep feeding our spirit with God's truth and love in our lives.

My husband struggled with unforgiveness with his cousin. He had a cousin who preyed on others and expected everybody to do everything for him. He was an addict and stole from his family members to support his drug habit. His cousin had a history of violent behavior from the drugs he was on. He had three different restraining orders from different women because of his anger from what the drugs were doing to his brain.

He made extremely poor decisions that caused lapse of sound judgment. In 2005 his cousin was living with his grandparents because his grandparents were trying to help him to get his life together. One day while his grandparents were not home due to traveling in their RV on a road trip, he went into the house and stole a Gibson guitar from his grandpa that was worth about $30,000 and sold it for a couple hundred dollars to support his drug addiction. He also stole all sorts of sports memorabilia, guns, and valuables.

This infuriated my husband that he did this to their grandpa, a sweet old man that would always do anything in the world for you. He took advantage of him and his loving and giving personality. Their grandfather is a strong and courageous man. He loves giving to church organizations, and sponsoring children overseas, political parties, and many different charitable companies to help feed the poor. You can see how generous of a person he is so there was no need for his grandson to do that to him.

When their grandfather got home he saw cocaine on the table and drug paraphernalia everywhere. Their grandfather was so upset. He kicked his grandson out of the house. Their grandfather had to go to all the pawn shops around town to collect the items that he pawned off and had to buy his own belongings back.

Their grandfather isn't in the greatest of health. He has many health issues. He has a bad heart. He was given eight months to live when my husband was eight years old. He has surpassed his life expectancy. He had at least thirty surgeries and six major heart attacks, and a dozen mini heart attacks that his defibrillator shocks his heart when he has a heart attack.

When my husband found out this happened it caused hatred in my husband's heart for many years. He didn't speak to his cousin after that. After years passed, finally his cousin got help, went to drug rehab, and attended ongoing AA meetings. He got off drugs and turned his life around. After my husband saw consistent better behavior his cousin reached out to him to apologize for his actions. Now they are finally in a good place and my husband forgave him for what he did.

Bitterness did take over my husband for a long time and he held a grudge against his cousin. This was one of the hardest parts for my husband to be able to let go and forgive. My husband is very protective of his family and when he saw his grandparents get hurt from his cousin's poor decisions it was extremely hard for him to let that anger go. My husband has moved past this now and has a relationship with his cousin.

They may not be as close as once before but at least they can be kind to each other and build a new bond of friendship.

It is incredibly important to forgive yourself and forgive others. It's also one of the most difficult things to do in life. It takes true strength to forgive someone who never apologized. Forgiving yourself for the shameful things you've done is not easy. I've had to forgive others who never apologized, and I've had to forgive myself for many shameful and regretful actions that I committed. But once I did, the weight was lifted off me and my heart became burden-free.

> In prayer there is a connection between what God does and what you do. You can't get forgiveness from God, for instance, without also forgiving others. If you refuse to do your part, you cut yourself off from God's part.
>
> Matthew 6:14-15, MSG

True happiness comes from the gift of forgiveness. Forgiving others and forgiving yourself only leads to the spirit of peace and joy. It takes courage to open your heart again after being hurt, but God rewards the ones who are courageous in his name. Have faith and do unto others the way you want others to do unto you. We all have hurt people, we all have committed selfish acts, and have done things we regret. Don't crucify and hold a grudge toward those who have hurt you.

O Master, these are the conditions in which people live, and yes, in these very conditions my spirit is still alive—fully recovered with a fresh infusion of life! It seems it was good for me to go through all those troubles. Throughout them all you held tight to my lifeline. You never let me tumble over the edge into nothing. But my sins you let go of, threw them over your shoulder—good riddance! The dead don't thank you, and choirs don't sing praises from the morgue. Those buried six feet under don't witness to your faithful ways. It's the living—live men, live women— who thank you, just as I'm doing right now. Parents give their children full reports on your faithful ways.

Isaiah 38:16-19, MSG

1 0

Celebration

Be cheerful with joyous celebration in every season of life. Let joy overflow, *for you are united with the Anointed One!* Let gentleness be seen in every relationship, for our Lord is ever near. Don't be pulled in different directions or worried about a thing. Be saturated in prayer throughout each day, offering your faith-filled requests before God with overflowing gratitude. Tell him every detail of your life, then God's wonderful peace that transcends human understanding, will make the answers known to you through Jesus Christ.

Phil 4:4-7 TPT

CELEBRATE JESUS' SACRIFICE FOR OUR LIVES

When we celebrate the Lord's Supper, we don't roast the lamb. The sacrifice has been made. We take the cup and remember that the blood of Christ was shed, and that by faith His blood is applied to your life. You are delivered from the wrath of God and brought out of the position you used to be in—a slave, and you are brought into the freedom of a new life with God, in which he says to you, "You are Mine, and I am yours." This is not a process—it's been accomplished. God gives you this feast, so you won't spend the rest of your life wondering if He loves you. You see that He loves you in the cross. God gives you this feast so that you won't spend the rest of your life wondering if you will be forgiven. You are forgiven in the cross, and faith sees that.

God gives you this feast so that you will not live the rest of your life as if you are still a slave. Through the Passover, God's people saw that God had put them in an entirely new position. No matter what your difficulties are in life, you are no longer a slave! This is what God says to us in the cross: You may face all kinds of battles in life, but you are not a slave! You are redeemed! You have been set free by the blood of Christ. Sin will always be your enemy, but it is no longer you master. That is worth celebrating![27]

In the past I may not have had a lot to celebrate, but I learned to seek joy in my life. I had to choose every day to make that conscious decision to overcome the heavy burdens in my life. I had to turn them back to God to use for good to bring joy in my walk. When I come into contact with people around me, they can experience that same type of joyful energy that my spirit was shining through me. This requires spiritual discipline to practice the heart of celebration, which creates strength in the mind. The more we pool our attention to focus on the choice of the higher things that matter in life, the more abundant amount of willpower we'll have to shake down the enemy when he tries to attack.

I remember a time in my life that the Spirit of Laughter came over me out of nowhere when I was in the car being picked up from work. Something came over me and I started to laugh and felt an overwhelming spirit of joy take over me. I couldn't stop laughing and it felt exhilarating. It was a feeling that I had never experienced before. My friend that was in the car with me started to laugh as well, and it went on for about ten minutes or so. When God's laughter comes through you it is a contagious feeling that others around you can experience at the same time. This is another way God shows His love through us so others can experience the same joy that God feels every day in Heaven.

I know that week I was fasting, praying, and meditating for God's direction. With my faithfulness fasting I feel God brought the angels down upon me and took my pain I was experiencing back to heaven and brought down the joy of laughter of the Holy Spirit. It felt so freeing. I felt my body being washed clean from all the disarray of messiness, disorder, and confusion that I was living. The Holy Spirit needed to set me free from my shackles of bondage.

Laughter in the Spirit is a faith-response by our spirit to God's victory through Christ over the devil. Laughter in the Spirit is a participation by the believer in the victory of Him of Whom it is written, "He who sits in the heavens shall laugh" (Psalm 2:4, NKJV).

Holy laughter is received by faith. It is an expression of faith, and it achieves what faith achieves. It causes God to procure victories on our behalf which He accomplishes by sending angels on our behalf. Examples of what takes place is joy, healing, freedom, revelation, profession, praise, thanksgiving, fellowship in the Spirit, prayer, intercession, petition, tongues, interpretations, prophecies, visions, exhortations, guidance, and instruction from the Spirit.

Fruit of the Holy Spirit, the Greek word καρπός that we translate "fruit", usually means fruit in the sense of edible fruits and vegetables. But it can also be translated as offspring, deed, action, result, or profit. In an agrarian society, fruit is a good thing; it is the result of hard work and careful tending. Today we might use the word "fruit" in a phrase such as the "fruit of our labor" to communicate the results of our efforts.

> But the fruit of the Spirit [the result of His presence within us] is love [unselfish concern for others], joy, [inner] peace, patience [not the ability to wait, but how we act while waiting], kindness, goodness, faithfulness, gentleness, self-control. Against such things there is no law. And those who belong to Christ Jesus have crucified the sinful nature together with its passions and appetites.
>
> Gal 5:22-24, AMP

THERE ARE 9 FRUITS OF THE SPIRIT

1. Love, the Greek word is Agape. It's the perfect love only God can give.

2. Joy is translated to delight. In the Bible it is seen as gladness. It is the realization of God's favor and grace in one's life. Biblical joy is happiness that is not dependent on our circumstances.

3. Peace is a life without conflict, as well as wholeness and harmony with God and others. It's a life of peace both physically and mentally.

4. Forbearance is translated using other words such as patience, endurance, constancy, steadfastness, perseverance, longsuffering, and slowness in avenging wrongs. The Holy Spirit empowers believers to withstand challenging situations with perseverance and endurance.

5. Kindness conveys the meaning of moral goodness, integrity, usefulness, and benignity. In the King James Version this word is translated "gentleness," which links it to the meaning of a gentleman or a gentlewoman, someone who behaved properly, with moral integrity and kindness.

6. Goodness means uprightness of heart and life, goodness, and kindness. Goodness is seen in our actions. This word relates to not only being good, but also doing good things.

7. Faithfulness evidence of the Holy Spirit's work in our lives. Faithfulness is a character trait that combines

dependability and trust based on our confidence in God and His eternal faithfulness.

8. Gentleness translated "meekness" in the King James Version, but because being meek seemed weak, modern translations of the Bible use gentleness to mean mildness of disposition.

9. Self-Control is the ability to control one's body and its sensual appetites and desires – physically and mentally – through the power of the Holy Spirit. Self-control relates to both chastity and sobriety, and particularly moderation in eating and drinking. Self-control is the opposite of the works of the flesh that indulge sensual desires.[28]

It's news I'm most proud to proclaim, this extraordinary Message of God's powerful plan to rescue everyone who trusts him, starting with Jews and then right on to everyone else! God's way of putting people right shows up in the acts of faith, confirming what Scripture has said all along: "The person in right standing before God by trusting him really lives.

Romans 1:16-17 MSG

CELEBRATION OF FRIENDSHIPS

Let's talk about Godly friendships that you need in your life. This is extremely important to have. I learned early on you cannot grow in God's direction without having supporting friendships by your side. As we grow in our walk with the Lord and learn to step up as leaders it is reassuring to have a friend there through your ups and downs. Sometimes you might be the strong one, then there are times your friend will be the strong encourager which is great to balance each other out when tough times come.

When a friend is in need it's important to step up your friendship and help your friend to get out of their pit of despair when they are weak. When we get tangled up in the fishing wire and can't seem to get ourselves out of it, it is so nice to have a friend there to cut you out or direct you out of the mess of the wire. I'd like to share a special moment finding Jesus Christ as my Lord and Savior with one of my best friends from my childhood. As I explained in one of my earlier chapters, we accepted Christ November 8, 1995 together. The bond between a friendship is amazing and never should be taken lightly.

Leading up to our acceptance of Christ in the summer in 1995 we were both searching and searching to fill a void in our hearts and lives. We were both broken. Her parents were divorced when she was nine years old and she had to go back and forth from her mom's to her dad's house. It was hard for her and her little sister. She felt torn from their parents not being together any longer. I had a troubled home with alcohol and verbally abusive father. We both needed each other and our friendship.

We both experienced heavy partying at a very young age. We were trying to find purpose and meaning. We were focused on all the wrong things by seeking popularity, being cool, alcohol, drugs, boys' attention, and fitting in, but this left us both still feeling empty and alone with no satisfaction of wholeness. When we were together hanging out we were like "two peas in a pod." We spent all our time together. I would go to her house and she would come to mine. We were two lost children trying to find love and hope in all the wrong places in life.

We got introduced to church by a great friend of mine, a boy I met in middle school. Him and another boy went to church a lot together. They would talk so positively about their church and I was super curious to learn more about it. They told me where they went and invited me to go. My best friend and I decided to go to church to see what all the fuss was about around October 1995. She remembered that we stood out the way we dressed compared to other girls in the group. We would dress up more than others and we had more revealing clothing, so we definitely stood out from the rest of the crowd.

We started to go there more and more because we liked what we heard and the girls there were so inviting and accepting of us in their group. About a month into going to church, one Sunday night our pastor was speaking and something powerful hit both of us and we knew we wanted to accept Jesus Christ in our hearts. We both walked up together to the altar and another girl walked with us and asked us if we wanted to pray. Her father was one of the pastors on staff. She was always so sweet and caring. She had an incredible spirit about her that I was instantly drawn too. I wanted to learn more of why she felt the way she did.

She prayed with both of us and led us to Christ right in front of the altar on our knees. I remember my best friend and I were bawling so much. We felt a strong chain lifted off our backs that had been holding us down. We immediately felt relief and excitement wash over us. When the service was over I remember people were congratulating us and we both felt loved and wanted. We knew there was something more to life. It hit us to the core and we knew this was it.

This was what we were missing that we had been searching for. We got baptized December 3, 1995. It was the best feeling ever. I remember being terrified to go up in front of the church with all the people there witnessing our act to choose Jesus. When we got dunked under and then rose out of the water I started to cry and felt an overwhelming peace in my soul. We found a new beginning of love with our Savior. This was the purest act of kindness that Jesus gave us.

I've told you these things for a purpose: that my joy might be your joy, and your joy wholly mature. This is my command: Love one another the way I loved you. This is the very best way to love. Put your life on the line for your friends. You are my friends when you do the things I command you. I'm no longer calling you servants because servants don't understand what their master is thinking and planning. No, I've named you friends because I've let you in on everything I've heard from the Father.

John 15:11-13, MSG

DEFINITION OF FRIENDSHIP

"Friendship means familiar and liking of each other's mind. People who are friends talk to each other and spend time together. They also help each other when they are in trouble or are hurt. The strength of the bond of friendship between two people can vary. If the bond is very strong, they are called best friends."[29]

I had another childhood friend who became one of my best friends with my other friend in elementary too. When my friend and I got saved we were so in love with Jesus and on fire with God. We started to share about Jesus to our other friends. We went to a church camp around June 1996. We had our friend go with us. It was an extraordinary experience that we never experienced before. It was one of the first church camps we attended at New Life Ranch in Colcord, OK after we got saved.

Ken Freeman was the speaker there. He is an evangelist who speaks to camps all around the world to share his passion about who Jesus Christ is. I remember that I had a connection to his story along with my other friend that we invited to camp. I grew up in a similar lifestyle as he did. He was the son of an alcoholic mother and an absentee father and experienced neglect. He experienced physical and sexual abuse as well. He lived a life with bitterness and pain as a child.

I related so much to his story it hit my soul deeply. My other friend who attended with us in camp was hit with the Holy Spirit and felt overwhelming pull and immediate longing to want to ask Christ into her heart as well. My beautiful friend asked Jesus into her heart. She was flooded with so much happiness. I treasured our friendship and was so thrilled for her to find Jesus. My heart melted. She grew up with an abusive, alcoholic father as well, who was also in and out of jail. We had a lot in common and we understood each other's struggles and pain. It was easy to talk with her because she knew exactly where my heart was coming from with all the pain of neglect and abuse we both experienced. I remember her father being in jail at the same time mine was when we graduated from high school. I truly appreciated our friendship.

Let's fast forward many years later after our acceptance of Christ. Both of my sisters in Christ had dinner with me when I visited back home to see my family (I no longer live in the same state as they do). It was a wonderful treat to spend time with them. The neatest thing was when we haven't seen each other in a very long time, our friendship doesn't skip a beat. We can pick up right where we left off because our bond is so close that it is easy to walk right back into our most vulnerable and sweet conversations. I am forever grateful to have both of them in my life. I know when times get tough, I can count on their friendship and the same goes for them. When they have struggles or sensitive topics that they are struggling with they know they can share their pain and know we are always there for one another without judgment.

Just as lotions and fragrance give sensual delight, a sweet friendship refreshes the soul.

Proverbs 27:9, MSG

Therefore encourage one another and build one another up, just as you are doing.

1 Thessalonians 5:11, ESV

CELEBRATE GODLY ACCOUNTABILITY FRIENDSHIPS

We all need someone in our life who holds us accountable with our walk in Christ even when we may not want someone to hold us up to a higher standard. However, it is extremely important to have someone that will be by your side and tell you when you have messed up. More importantly to encourage you by speaking life over you and telling you to get back up when you fall or make mistakes. When we mature with our faith, it's important to have friends by your side that will lift you up instead of becoming a hindrance in your walk with Christ. This is important for your spiritual growth. Being held accountable may seem frustrating at times but this is essential to help you find your spiritual gifts that God has given you; to walk in wisdom and learn the fundamentals of true Biblical advice with grace-filled accountability.

Later in my adult life I met an amazing woman of God through my husband. She worked in the same work area as he worked. He met her in a coffee line at work around December 2014. He liked how kind she was and knew she was someone I would love to be friends with. My husband met her husband one day when he came to pick up his wife from work to drive back home. My husband really liked her husband and they hit it off quickly.

They invited us to come to their home with our three children to spend a day fishing and cooking out with them and their three kids. This was May 2, 2015. This was a turning point in our friendship. I remember meeting them for the first time and I loved their spirit. I immediately felt love and they were kindhearted people that loved Jesus. Throughout my life, I hadn't met many women that loved Jesus and were all around down to earth people. Their entire family radiated joy and favor of God. I loved how their family represented what spiritual family looks like with complete joy, laughter, gentleness with one another and true love.

When I saw how beautiful their marriage was it helped me to see what true love represented. This gave me a glimpse of my future with my husband and our three small children as they get older. They had a calmness about them. I knew I wanted to have that same type of marriage with my husband as we get older where, after being married for more than twenty years we'd still being in love and flirt with one another. They are great role models to show what a marriage should look like.

It was always so adorable to watch how they played with each other. Their love was the purest form from our Heavenly Father. It gave me excitement to look forward to with my husband. We had only been married for seven years at the time. The more we hung out with them, the closer our friendship grew. We went on vacations, had slumber parties, took the boat out, spent holidays together, and went on adventures. I cherished every moment I had with them.

I know one special moment I grew closer to my sweet friend was when my husband went into the hospital for pain in his stomach. It ended up being more serious and his appendix was rupturing so they had to rush him into surgery to remove it. I had small children at the time. I left my children with a babysitter while my friend went with me to the hospital and spent time with me waiting for my husband to get out of surgery. I was so scared. I remembered when we were waiting, she opened up to me on hurts she had experienced in her past. She was hurting in her soul with a best friend she had that ended up being someone who really wasn't a friend at all and stopped being friends with her for no reason. It hurt her soul so badly she didn't understand what she did to her friend that would cause her to stop being friends with her all of a sudden.

She couldn't wrap her mind why her friend would do that to her. She was in so much pain from the rejection and the not knowing why. This truly affected her soul so profoundly. She tried to speak to her friend only to find rejection from her and she ignored her in the hallways at work. My friend was so thankful that I was not like this and that I was someone who truly cared for her through all of her good and bad moments. We became each other's accountability partner. She was fighting against the burnout, trying to make sense of everything. I wanted to be there for her so her spiritual growth would not suffer from the mental and emotional exhaustion. I wanted to be a listening ear and help encourage her to bring her back centered with the gospel and give her peace that she had a godly friend who cared for her and wanted to bring her out of the pain that was tormenting her soul.

I learned it's important when you have a friend who is tired and feeling downright awful they need that support system to help give them a break from what they are experiencing. Life can be messy and requires a great deal of patience, gentleness, and speaking the truth in love to a friend. We need wisdom from God. God will put wisdom in us to help a friend out in need by speaking grace over them. We cannot do ministry alone. Each one of us has strengths and weaknesses in our ministry walk.

On the flip side I was in a moment of weakness and hurt as well. My marriage went into shambles when we moved from Kansas to New Mexico. My sweet beautiful friend was by my side even when I was hundreds of miles away. She spoke to me every day and spoke encouraging words. She helped me to get out of the pit of despair. I was tangled up in bitterness, resentment, confusion, and anger. I was heartbroken, lost, sick to my stomach, drained, and overwhelm with sadness when my husband and I were separated for a short time.

I felt truly like I had lost a loved one. I felt tormented with pain and anxiety. It literally felt like my husband died. One moment you think everything is fine and the next moment your soul was ripped out of your body. I never felt so much hurt in my life. I was lost but I had an amazing friend who was supportive and helped me to get through the nightmare I was experiencing.

Through her faithfulness, prayer, and listening ear she spoke love to me and it helped me to fight my pain one day at a time. It encouraged me to fight for my marriage. I would pray, meditate, and speak in tongues quietly with my long hours of prayer in the middle of the night. God woke me up many times around 3:00 a.m. praying for my husband and rebuking the enemy that was trying to steal my husband away from God's hand. I was more determined than ever to cast the devil out of my husband's mind. My husband was battling the enemy and I knew God was telling me to keep praying for my husband and his soul over and over.

When I needed a friend to be by my side through my anguish, she was there for me. I appreciated the love she spoke over me along with her husband. She experienced similar hurts too with this process. Our family was so close that it even affected her and her husband. Through their faithfulness and constant prayer my husband and I made it out of the pit. Praise Jesus!

Prayer:

Lord, I ask that you bless all my beautiful friends that are out there. I pray you reward them with their faithfulness and the abundance of love they have in their hearts. Thank you for blessing them with a loving heart that is pure with your grace. I ask for your favor to be with them through the good and bad. When they feel at the lowest point in their life, help them to grab a hold of you tight so they don't get stuck in their walk with you. Take away the clouds that are hovering over their eyes that prevent them from seeing the amazing plan You have in store for them. I know many of them are struggling right now. Help them to see the light at the end of the tunnel. Give them peace and reassurance that this season of frustration, discouragement, rejection, the not knowing what their future holds, uncomfortableness what is happening to them this very moment will soon pass and the reward for their lives is just right around the corner that You bestowed for them. Give them clear vision, so they can see what You are trying to show them. In Jesus Mighty Name Amen.

There will be people that will need you in their lives. You may have friends that are going through a divorce, or went through one, lost their job or meaning/purpose for their life, lost a loved one, suffered broken friendships, financial problems, sexual abuse, rape, physical abuse from a spouse currently or previously in their past, suicidal thoughts or drug/alcohol abuse. We must be there for our friends. We cannot do this alone in life. It is very important to have accountability partners in your path that can encourage you to get through the pain you have experienced or are currently experiencing now.

If we cannot give someone hope in life, on their current outcome they are in, this can lead a person to take their own life if they feel like they're backed into a corner and cannot get out. I have had many people in my life that have taken their own life because they felt like it was their only option to get out of the wretched pain they were in. Most people believe if they end their life that it will end their pain/suffering that they are in, but they don't realize they leave a ripple effect behind. If they have a spouse, children, siblings, parents, cousins, aunts and uncles this hurts everyone who was a part of that person's life.

BEAR ONE ANOTHER'S BURDENS

Brothers, if anyone is caught in any sin, you who are spiritual [that is, you who are responsive to the guidance of the Spirit] are to restore such a person in a spirit of gentleness [not with a sense of superiority or self-righteousness], keeping a watchful eye on yourself, so that you are not tempted as well. Carry one another's burdens and in this way you will fulfill the requirements of the law of Christ [that is, the law of Christian love]. For if anyone thinks he is something [special] when [in fact] he is nothing [special except in his own eyes], he deceives himself.

Galatians 6:1-3, AMP

CELEBRATE YOUR MARRIAGE

Marriages take work, commitment, and love, but they also need respect to be truly happy and successful. A marriage based on love and respect doesn't just happen. Both spouses have to do their part.

Husbands, love your wives [seek the highest good for her and surround her with a caring, unselfish love], just as Christ also loved the church and gave Himself up for her, so that He might sanctify the church, having cleansed her by the washing of water with the word [of God], so that [in turn] He might present the church to Himself in glorious splendor, without spot or wrinkle or any such thing; but that she would be holy [set apart for God] and blameless. Even so husbands should and are morally obligated to love their own wives as [being in a sense] their own bodies. He who loves his own wife loves himself. For no one ever hated his own body, but [instead] he nourishes and protects and cherishes it, just as Christ does the church, because we are members (parts) of His body. FOR THIS REASON A MAN SHALL LEAVE HIS FATHER AND HIS MOTHER AND SHALL BE JOINED [and be faithfully devoted] TO HIS WIFE, AND THE TWO SHALL BECOME ONE FLESH. This mystery [of two becoming one] is great; but I am speaking with reference to [the relationship of] Christ and the church. However, each man among you [without exception] is to love his wife as his very own self [with behavior worthy of respect and esteem, always seeking the best for her with an attitude of lovingkindness], and the wife [must see to it] that she respects and delights in her husband [that she notices him and prefers him and treats him with loving concern, treasuring him, honoring him, and holding him dear].

Ephesians 5:25-33, AMP

Communicate clearly and often

"Talking with your spouse is one of the best ways to keep your marriage healthy and successful. Be honest about what you're feeling but be kind and respectful when you communicate. Part of good communication is being a good listener and taking the time to understand what it is your spouse wants and needs from you. Keep the lines of communication open by talking often, and not just about things like bills and the kids. Share your thoughts and feelings.

Tell your spouse that you're thankful for having him or her in your life.

Appreciate each other, your relationship, your family, and your lives together. Show gratitude when your partner cooks dinner, helps the kids with their homework, or does the grocery shopping. It may help to take a few minutes each evening to tell each other at least one thing you appreciated that day.

Make time for you two as a couple

With work and family responsibilities, it can be easy to lose the romance factor. Plan special dates, either to go out or just stay at home. If you have children, send them on a play date while you relax, talk, and enjoy each other's company.

PLAN FOR SOME PERSONAL TIME

Alone time is just as important as couple time. Everyone needs time to recharge, think, and enjoy personal interests. That time is often lost when you're married, especially if you have kids. Go out with friends, take a class, or do volunteer work, whatever you find enriching. When you're back together with your spouse, you'll appreciate each other even more.

Understand that it's OK to disagree

You won't agree on everything, but it is important to be fair and respectful during disagreements. Listen to your spouse's point of view. Try not to get angry and don't let yourself become too frustrated. Walk away and calm down if you need to, then discuss the problem again when you're both in a better frame of mind. Compromise on problems so that you both give a little.

BUILD TRUST

Marriage therapist and researcher John Gottman, Ph.D., has found that criticism, contempt, defensiveness, and stonewalling are serious threats to a marriage. The more a couple engages in these destructive activities, the more likely they are to divorce. His decades of research and of working with couples have shown that spouses who stay together know how to fight without being hostile and to take responsibility for their actions. They are also more likely to respond quickly to each other's wishes to make up after fights and repair the relationship.

LEARN TO FORGIVE

Everyone makes mistakes. Your spouse may hurt your feelings or do something that upsets you, and that may make you angry, even furious. But it's important to deal with your feelings, let them go, and move on. Don't keep bringing up the past.

Remember to remain committed to your spouse, your family, and the life that you have built together. Support each other emotionally and in everyday ways. You, your spouse, and your relationship may grow and change with time, but these ideas can help your marriage stay successful over the years.[30]

This is a great article to read that sums up the simplest things you can do to be successful throughout your marriage.

My husband and I try to spend as much quality time as we are able to with having such busy schedules. His job is extremely dangerous being a Chief of Police for the BIA. He has been in many scary situations. I thank God every day that He brings him back home safe and sound to us. He sees a lot of neglect and abuse where he works. Sometimes he has a hard time letting go of what he sees at work. When he comes home from work it can be difficult for him to leave behind the outcome of trying situations of his day like sexual assaults, drug and alcohol abuse, neglect, people getting in wrecks from drinking or huffing fumes from hairspray, murder, etc.

He tries to clear his mind before he walks in from a long day at work. It has carried into our family time many nights. It can be difficult for him to balance being in a high-demand position. He does the best he can from what he is able to do with our time. I try to be very understanding and supportive. When he does slow down from a stressful day he enjoys his family coming to greet him with a big hug and kiss when he walks in. It means everything to him. If we forget to come or don't notice him coming in it really hurts his soul. He has expressed to me the most important thing that he values with myself and the children is our love and appreciation for him.

When he has a tough day, it brings joy to his face knowing he is loved at home and that we value what he does when he is away on duty at his shift. I want to build him up not tear him down. If he doesn't feel like his family cares, it does bring his spirit down and causes sadness in his heart. I want to be the best wife that I can be for him. I am not perfect, but I do cherish my husband tremendously.

We both enjoy when all the kids are asleep, and it is just him and I in our room. We cuddle, flirt with each other, act silly and laugh. We have pillow talk and hold each other's hand before we fall asleep. We either face each other when falling asleep or he holds me at night in his arms. This is the best feeling for both of us knowing we have our love for one and another. When we know we've had a bad day at work, the kids are not listening at home, or someone is trying to bring us down, we know we have each other's support and listening ear.

Another thing that helps our marriage to be strong is throughout the day my husband and I will call each other at work just to show our love, even if it is just a quick second to say "hi" and "how is your day going?" It gives my husband juice to finish his day strong knowing I am thinking about him throughout the day. He loves when I call him in the morning when I start my day just to wish him a great day and to be safe. I also will check in with him in the middle of the day to see how he is doing and make sure he is safe and okay mentally. There might be days that I get so busy, or he does as well, and we may not get to call each other until the end of the day. I know when I don't call him, it bothers him, and he loves hearing my voice. I am not perfect by any means and will slip and forget to call. I know this hurts my husband.

With this all being said, cherish your spouse. You need each other, and God meant for marriage to be one-not separate. This may seem a little silly to you, but it works wonders in our marriage to keep it strong and alive. Find what is important to your spouse so you can work on things that make you both happy. Just doing simple things for your spouse really does change the dynamic of your relationship and set a tone in your marriage. Celebrate your spouse and all they do, along with appreciating them with acts of kindness, or their love language. Get out of your comfort zone by showing your spouse you hear their hurts, or what they are missing from you. Show them by actions, not just words, that you will do it, and really hear them.

Focus on your spouse's strengths rather than their weaknesses, encourage and lift them up instead of criticizing them. Be loyal to your spouse. God designed a marriage to mirror His covenant relationship between man and woman.

Praise:

Thank you, my precious King, for blessing me with my soul mate. He is an incredible man. I love and adore all his attributes. Thank you for him challenging me in areas that I needed to be challenged on to grow in my walk with You and my marriage with him. Thank You for his extraordinary strength and his courageous heart fighting for our country, community, innocent children, our kids, and me. Thank You for him being "one of the kind men" that is confident who he is. Thank You, Jesus, for giving him an amazing, sensitive heart that I cherish profoundly. I love all the strength and weakness. Thank You for him being a natural born leader within our family and outside of our family. Thank You, God, for blessing him to be a wonderful father to our three beautiful children. Most of all I am thankful for his loving spirit that wants to see the best in me, and I am grateful for him loving and choosing me to be his wife.

CELEBRATING YOUR CHILDREN

Don't you see that children are GOD's best gift? The fruit of the womb his generous legacy? Like a warrior's fistful of arrows are the children of a vigorous youth. Oh, how blessed are you parents, with your quivers full of children! Your enemies don't stand a chance against you; you'll sweep them right off your doorstep.

Psalm 127:3-5, MSG

God calls children a blessing and a gift. Jesus tells us to be like children and to come to Him full of faith and trust. Children are innocent and tender-hearted.

My husband and I have a sweet, sensitive eight-year-old boy who is so in touch with his feelings. When he sees commercials of dogs or children that have been neglected, he will immediately start crying and want to save them all. It breaks my heart because it truly affects him so deeply that he will cry for hours about it. He has such a caring and loving heart.

One time my husband, our children, and I were eating dinner. We left the restaurant and it was super cold outside and snowing heavily. Keep in mind, we live in North Dakota. This state is super cold and gorgeous at the same time with the beauty of God's reflection in the white snow. We pulled out and noticed an older lady walking on the sidewalk with a hood over her head. Something pulled at my husband's spirit and tugged on my sons' hearts when they saw her. She looked like she was freezing. We pulled up next to her to see if she was okay. We asked her if she needed a ride. She was so appreciative and happy that we asked, and she agreed.

We asked her where she was heading. She needed something at CVS so we took her, and she said she could get a ride back from there. On the way there my two sons were so curious and asking her personal questions. I told them to stop but they kept asking where her car was and her family. My two sons were deeply moved. It was so adorable to see how their innocent souls work. It reminded me what Jesus would do in that situation.

My boys were so worried about her, especially my eight-year-old. When we pulled up to the store my husband gave her some money that he had in his pocket before she got out of the car. She was so thankful. When we were dropping her off, my son started to cry when she got out of the car. He was watching her walk into the store. We drove off. Everyone in the car was so sad for her. We left her at CVS and my son was bawling and was so sad that she didn't have a car and she was poor living on the streets. He was so worried about her. We felt like that wasn't enough for her. My husband felt like she needed more help. We didn't feel right leaving her there, so we turned around and went back to the store.

My husband asked my son if he wanted to go in with him to the store to give her more money and he was so happy. It calmed him down some to go in to help the older woman out. He was the one that handed her the money. She was shocked and thankful. They asked her if they could give her a ride back to where she needed to go. She agreed once again to allow us to help her out. We took her where she was staying. It saddened us because where she was staying was in her car. She reassured us everything was okay. It was a temporary thing. Her car was parked at an apartment complex and she had friends staying there and she was going to be fine. We said our goodbyes to her. This was hard for all of us to see but it was an incredible teachable moment for our children to experience what it is like to help someone else out who is in need.

It's important to teach your children humility and the fundamentals they need to have in life to become successful with their walk with Christ. Celebrate them when they do something courageous.

> Teach a child how to follow the right way; even when he is old, he will stay on course.
>
> Proverbs 22:6, VOICE

My sweet eleven-year-old daughter wanted to share a story here that touched her heart. These are her words that she wrote to me.

> It all started when I was in second grade. I was eight years old. I had a boy in my class that has special needs and is Autistic. He would get stressed with loud sounds. When he would get agitated, I would go over there to help him out. I would interact and talk to him calmly and he would settle down. I loved how he trusted me and even more so than our teachers. I would talk with him in a calm voice and spoke encouraging words to him. It made his day. He would turn happy right away. Anytime he had an episode I would walk up to him and he had a huge grin on his face and immediately would be happy again. My teacher started to notice this, so she put him right next to me

in class. Anytime he would get upset I would talk to him with ease and love. There were times he would get so upset in class he started to throw the desks and chairs at people. He hit me on my leg, and he noticed I was hurt when I was putting pressure on my leg when it hurt me. He immediately ran up to me and was begging me to tell him if I was okay and to forgive him. He started getting tears in his eyes and felt so bad that he hurt me that he started bawling. I gave him a hug and told him I am alright. He cared for me so much that he walked with me down to the nurse's office to make sure I was fine. It made him feel better knowing I was okay if he was able to be right by my side while I was being checked out by the nurse.

There was another time that really changed me. I saw he was getting bullied by a group of kids. He tried his best to stand up for himself but didn't succeed. The group of people threw his headphones over the fence during recess where we are not allowed to go. I ran over there yelling at them to "Go away and leave him alone!" Once I got over there, I got scared thinking in my head, what did I just say? The group of people said to me, "what are you going to do princess?" I spoke back said, "1. Don't call me princess. 2. I can get the teacher. 3. He is my friend!!" I grabbed the boy's hand and walked away and went toward the teachers. The group of kids ran off. My sweet friend gave me a big hug. I jumped over the fence and got his headphones back for him which we are not allowed to do but, in my heart, I knew that was the right thing to do all considering what just happened to him.

This was a touching moment for me. I am getting tears in my eyes just thinking back to that moment. He has touched my heart in so many ways. I learned to stand up for others and myself that are in need. No one should ever be bullied. My parents taught me to stand up for what I believe in and especially for the helpless that cannot defend themselves. They taught me to be a strong independent girl and to be a leader not a follower. I know who I am and that is a child of God. No one should ever deserve to be made fun of or be put down because they have special needs. It taught me to be a voice for others and to do all I can to stop bullying. Thank you for listening to my story."

"Don't let even one rotten word seep out of your mouths. Instead, offer only fresh words that build others up when they need it most. That way your good words will communicate grace to those who hear them.

Eph 4:29, VOICE

My youngest child is a six-year-old boy. He has been in Christian schools since he was two. He loves going to school and learning about Jesus. He consistently reminds us on Sundays that we have church. He gets so excited to go. He gets upset and disappointed on days when we miss church. He says, "We can't miss church. We need to learn about Jesus." It's so cute. He is still very young and has a lot to learn. He holds me accountable on days when I am lazy from a long week of work where I may want to skip church to relax and take a day off to rest. He says, "Mommy we can't miss church. We need to go so I can learn."

It makes me feel so terrible on the days we miss it and tell him we cannot go. I feel so guilty when he has that disappointed face. One of his favorite things to do is draw me pictures. He can draw for hours and loves to show me his pictures that he drew. It makes him sad if he cannot show me his project he learned from church and what he drew from the Bible story he learned. It breaks my heart. He is my strong-willed child. He is very smart for his age.

At bedtime, he loves to pray. We have to pray three times. It cracks me up. I pray to him, then he repeats my prayer that I have him say and he says his own prayer. He has to do this every night. He cannot go to sleep unless we do this. When we are done he has to kiss my cheek two times each on each side and he wants me to do the same, and then we have to hug twice. I love it. It makes my heart melt. It is extremely adorable.

He is still very young, so he hasn't experienced many things yet. I will say, one thing he does struggle with is sharing his toys. He has gotten much better, but we had to redirect him a lot to make sure he shares his toys with his brother or his peers at school. He would get so caught up in playing with a specific toy that he would struggle to let go of it and let one of his friends at school play with it. He tries to take ownership of it when it is a classroom toy. We had to teach him to practice taking turns. When he would give a toy up to his brother or peers, we would praise him, and this gave him encouragement to do it more and more.

When he first started to go to school, he had another child bite him a lot if he took his toys. He would come home with bite marks and bruises from the child not understanding how to share as well. It was an ongoing issue for about a year, then my son started to get the hang of it. We wanted to teach our child to be a giver, not to take away from others. If we can learn to instill this early in their minds at a young age I believe this will give them the right tools later on in life to help others that are in need.

We must teach our children early on to have a compassionate heart, and encourage generosity and humility for others. When we are confronted to have compassion for others through their own sufferings, we can find it difficult to give our own time to give love and a listening ear. However, helping others with their physical needs, not only their spiritual needs, is a fundamental principle of Christian spirituality. Perhaps it would be easier to have a generous heart if we could turn away our own continual consumptions and live simpler lifestyles. Then there would be not only willingness but also the ability to share God's blessings with others. When we give back it is important because our feelings of compassion, humanity, and sense of appreciation awakens our souls when we give to others. Giving really is better than receiving. Grace is the highest form of generosity.

But I will say this *to encourage your generosity*: the one who plants little harvests little, and the one who plants plenty harvests plenty. Giving grows out of the heart—otherwise, you've reluctantly grumbled "yes" because you felt you had to or because you couldn't say "no," *but this isn't the way God wants it.* For *we know that* "God loves a cheerful giver." God is ready to overwhelm you with more blessings than you could ever imagine so that you'll always be taken care of in every way and you'll have more than enough to share.

2 Cor 9:6-8, VOICE

It was a pleasure to share my story with you. I pray God will use my vulnerabilities, hurts, and struggles in my past and present to be able to give you hope and encouragement for you to be an overcomer. Thank you for being a listening ear. Stay strong even when you feel defeated. God will bless and reward you for all you do.

About the Author

During my twelve years of marriage to my husband, I have been an Army wife. Then after my husband was injured, I became the wife of a Wounded Warrior, and now I am a Police wife with him serving as a Chief of Police. I am proud to be the mother of three amazing children, ages 6, 8, and 11. I have spent my life trying to find ways to serve the Lord through my businesses that I started and operated for over fifteen years through volunteering to mentor young ladies or serve in other capacities.

Nikki A. Edwards

Notes

1 https://www.lexico.com/en/synonym/agony

2 https://www.lexico.com/en/synonym/protector; https://www.lexico.com/en/synonym/guardian; https://www.lexico.com/en/synonym/defender

3 *Dictionary.com, LLC.* Last modified 2019. https://www.dictionary.com/browse.

4 Dr. Jeanne King, "Narcissistic Politics in Intimate Relationships," *Partners in Prevention*, last modified 2019, http://www.enddomesticabuse.org/article_narcissistic_politics_abuse_signs_524.php?gclid=EAIaIQobChMIxsWk1e764QIVA73sCh1yswFfEAAYASAAEgJnHfD_BwE.

5 DBSA, "DBSAlliance.org," *Depression and Bipolar Support Alliance*, March 31, 2019, https://www.dbsalliance.org/education/bipolar-disorder/diagnosis/?gclid=EAIaIQobChMI8I3ooIj-4QIVUvDACh3n1wgkEAAYBCAAEgKiqvD_BwE.

6 Got Questions Ministries, "Why did Amnon rape Tamar? Why didn't David punish Amnon?" February 15, 2017, https://www.gotquestions.org/Amnon-and-Tamar.html.

7 NIDA, "Health Consequences of Drug Misuse," March 23, 2017, https://www.drugabuse.gov/publications/health-consequences-drug-misuse/neurological-effects.

8 Jeffrey Juergens, "Addiction Center is Now Honcode Certified," August 26, 2015, https://www.addictioncenter.com/addiction/addiction-brain.

9 Elizabeth W. McGolerick, "Dad Texts Daughter Reasons He Loves Her Mom, We All Swoon," February 9, 2017, https://www.sheknows.com/parenting/articles/821928/the-importance-of-the-father-daughter-relationship-2.

10 Perry, J. C. (1996). "Dependent personality disorder". In Gabbard, Glen O.; Atkinson, Sarah D. (eds.). *Synopsis of Treatments of Psychiatric Disorders*. American Psychiatric Press. pp. 995–8, https://en.wikipedia.org/wiki/Dependent_personality_disorder.

11 Got Questions Ministries, "What does the Bible say about PTSD?" February 15, 2017, https://www.gotquestions.org/Bible-PTSD.html.

12 American Academy of Pediatrics. Healthychildren.org (2018, April 13). Child Abuse and Neglect. https://www. healthychildren.org/English/safety-prevention/at-home/ Pages/What-to-Know-about-Child-Abuse.aspx.

13 Terry, M., Sweeny, K. & Shepperd, J. (2007). Self-presentation. In R. F. Baumeister & K. D. Vohs (Eds.), *Encyclopedia of Social Psychology* (Vol. 1, pp. 836-838). Thousand Oaks, CA: SAGE Publications, Inc. doi: 10.4135/9781412956253. n494. https://sk.sagepub.com/reference/socialpsychology/ n494.xml.

14 WebMD Medical. Bhandari, Smitha MD. (2019, May 15) What Are PTSD Triggers? https://www.webmd.com/ mental-health/what-are-ptsd-triggers#2.

15 Bloom, Jon. (2015, July 15) desiringGod. Breaking the Power of Shame. https://www.desiringgod.org/articles/breaking-the-power-of-shame#hiding-in-the-wrong-place.

16 SparkNotes Editors. "SparkNote on Bible: The Old Testament." SparkNotes.com. SparkNotes LLC. 2002. Web. 5 Sept. 2019. https://www.sparknotes.com/lit/oldtestament/ section11.

17 Provided by TherapistAid.com (2016) Therapist Aid LLC. Retrieved from S:\Handouts\Clinical\Relationships; Personal Boundaries.pd.

18 Vaisman, Dr Boris. (2018, March 5). "Seasons In Malibu World Class Addiction Treatment. Is Compulsive Lying a Personality Disorder?" https://seasonsmalibu.com/is-compulsive-lying-a-personality-disorder.

19 Mental Health America. (2019). Co-Dependency. Characteristics of Co-Dependent People. https://www.mentalhealthamerica.net/co-dependency.

20 Break the Cycle volunteer, Liz. (2014), Dating Violence Blog. Setting Boundaries in a Relationship, https://www.breakthecycle.org/blog/setting-boundaries-relationship.

21 Parker, Dr Jonathan. (2018 May 25). Dr Jonathan Parker Spiritual Affirmations for Spiritual Healing and Transformation, https://www.jonathanparker.org/affirmations/spiritual-affirmations-for-spiritual-healing-and-transformation.

22 Kirby, Stephanie. (2019 August 1). Betterhelp. "Signs of Low Self-Esteem And What To Do About It," https://www.betterhelp.com/advice/self-esteem/signs-of-low-self-esteem-and-what-to-do-about-it.

23 Laurie Meyers, "A struggle for hope" February 2007, Vol 38, No. 2, Print version: p.30 https://www.apa.org/monitor/feb07/astruggle.

24 By the MindTools Content Team. (2018). "Building Self-Confidence: Prepare Yourself for Success!" https://www.mindtools.com/selfconf.html.

25 Manfred F. R. Kets de Vries, "Are You a Victim of the Victim Syndrome?" https://sites.insead.edu/facultyresearch/research/doc.cfm?did=50114.

26 George, Cylon. Huffpost "The Blog 10 Ways to Stop Feeling Like A Victim Once and for All," September 25, 2015, https://www.huffpost.com/entry/10-ways-to-stop-feeling-l_b_8193216.

27 Bunyan, John, "Unlocking the Bible Take Two: The Power of a Fresh Start. Celebrate All That is Yours in Christ," October 24, 2010, https://unlockingtheBible.org/sermon/celebrate-all-that-is-yours-in-christ.

28 Noyes, Penney, "What Are the Fruits of the Spirit?" Christianity.com, February 26, 2019, https://www.christianity.com/wiki/holy-spirit/what-are-the-fruits-of-the-spirit.html.

29 Wikipedia, "Friendship," August 7, 2019, https://simple.wikipedia.org/wiki/Friendship.

30 University of Rochester Medical Center. Health Encyclopedia. (2019). https://www.urmc.rochester.edu/encyclopedia/content.aspx?contenttypeid=1&contentid=4580.

CPSIA information can be obtained
at www.ICGtesting.com
Printed in the USA
FSHW011810141119